SHEEPDOG LIBERALISM

Sheepdog Liberalism

by

Jonathan Aibi

Sheepdog Liberalism

Disclaimer

This book presents the author's perspective and analysis on contemporary political dynamics, public institutions, and systems of power. It does not claim neutrality, nor does it represent the official position of any organization, employer, agency, or political body. The interpretations and arguments expressed herein are intentional, reasoned, and the product of independent thought.

Facts, statistics, and historical references have been drawn from sources deemed reliable at the time of writing; however, political conditions evolve. Readers are urged to investigate, verify, and think critically, rather than accept any position, including the author's, without scrutiny.

This work is not a substitute for legal advice, policy directives, or professional guidance. Neither the author nor the publisher assumes liability for actions taken or conclusions drawn based on the ideas presented. The responsibility for civic judgment rests, as it always has, with the reader.

Foreword

This book was written in response to a clear and measurable decline in liberal conviction within the United Kingdom.

The liberal tradition that once defined British politics, founded on individual freedom, civic duty, pluralism, and restraint of power, has weakened.

In its place, stronger and more absolutist ideologies have gained ground.

Populism, religious extremism, and ideological puritanism now threaten the social balance that liberal democracy requires to survive.

Sheepdog Liberalism sets out a direct answer to that crisis.

It presents a framework for the renewal of liberalism as a civic and moral project, not merely a political label.

It argues that liberty cannot endure without defence, that open societies require vigilance, and that tolerance cannot mean surrender to those who wish to destroy or overthrow it.

The chapters that follow trace the erosion of Britain's liberal institutions, examine the rise of movements that exploit their weakness, and outline the path by which liberalism can renew and fortify itself with courage, strength, and justice.

This work does not seek to invent liberalism anew, but to recover its discipline, restore its confidence, and return it to service of the nation it once led.

Sheepdog

[noun]

- A dog trained to guard and herd sheep.
- A guardian of the flock of Liberalism, any citizen who stands watch to protect the freedom they share.

VOLUME I: The Soul

Liberalism has been the sheep for too long. Proud of its softness, gentle with its enemies, it has wandered further and further into the valley while wolves gather in the tree line.

The sheep says, "*We all breathe the same air. We can all live together.*"

The wolves agree. Until night falls.

Sheepdog Liberalism is not the sheep. And it is not the wolf.

It is what stands between them.

Loyal. Watchful. It does not look for a fight, but it knows what happens when you ignore danger.

The sheepdog is not cruel. But it is not soft.

It barks before threats grow. It holds the line when others scatter.

It steps forward. Not from hunger, but from duty.

Liberalism must remember how to defend itself.

Not with paranoia. Not with vengeance. But with courage, structure, and strength.

Because without those who stand watch, freedom becomes just a story we used to tell.

The Philosophy: Liberal Values Are British Values

Sheepdog Liberalism is not just a political stance. It is a moral inheritance.

It is the soul of Britain, shaped by struggle, refined by principle, and passed down not through blood, but through belief.

To be British is not to cling to empire or nostalgia. It is to carry the torch of liberty. To uphold fairness. To defend the rule of law. To protect the rights of the individual, even when it is hard. Even when it is unpopular.

These are not borrowed values. They were born in British soil.

They were carved into the Magna Carta, a medieval sword raised not for conquest, but for rights.

They were forged in the fires of the Enlightenment, in coffee houses, universities, and parliaments where ideas challenged kings and truth defied orthodoxy.

They were written in the blood price paid to end slavery. A system this nation dismantled at global scale, not because it was profitable, but because it was right.

They were sung by suffragettes, fought for in the streets of the labour movement, and upheld through bombs and blackouts when Britain stood alone against fascism and did not flinch.

This is the liberal tradition of Britain.

Not weakness. Not naivety.

Conviction. Sacrifice. Justice.

Ours is a country where voices from every colour, creed, and class have joined the national story. Not by erasing difference, but by defending shared dignity.

We do not fear diversity. We fear division.

And so, we built a nation where laws protect all, where government serves the citizen, and where freedom is not a luxury, but a birthright.

This is what it means to be British.

And it is what Sheepdog Liberalism exists to defend with clarity, courage, and conviction.

Because these values are not abstract.

They are not automatic.
They are not guaranteed.
They must be taught. Lived. Protected.

And when challenged, they must be fought for.

Not with cruelty. Not with vengeance. But with unshakable pride in the society we have built, and a fierce refusal to see it destroyed.

When Freedom Becomes Invisible

Modern liberals have forgotten the price we paid for our rights.

We speak of rights as if they are natural, inevitable, the starting point of any decent society. But history tells a different story.

The right of women to vote. The right of gay people to marry. The right to speak freely, believe freely, live freely.

These were not handed down. They were fought for. And in much of the world, they still do not exist.

Liberalism assumed it had won the moral argument. That equality, fairness, and autonomy would become the natural defaults of civilisation.

It was wrong.

And in that assumption, we stopped teaching the case for liberty.

We stopped explaining why equality matters; not just morally, but practically.

That when you let everyone participate, regardless of identity, gender, political belief, you don't just feel good about it.

You build a society that is richer, smarter, stronger, more humane, and more stable.

Liberalism raised living standards, extended life expectancy, lowered infant mortality, and triggered revolutions in science, art, and culture.

It is the only system that lets a society disagree without

bloodshed, evolve without collapse, and include without erasing its core.

But now, when wolves enter the public square calling for obedience over equality, mocking liberalism as weakness, and reducing citizens to subjects, we are often silent.

We have forgotten the argument. We assumed the fight was over.

It isn't.

And now, a generation raised in the comfort liberalism built has started to bite the very hand that fed it.

It mistakes safety for stagnation. Openness for weakness.

Sheepdog Liberalism exists to remind them:

Liberalism did not win by default.

It was chosen, again and again by those who knew exactly what came without it.

And worse, in forgetting the fight, we turned the critique of liberalism into a chorus against it. A burden unique to free societies.

The Burden of Critique

Liberalism carries a strange burden. Because it allows critique, it receives critique. Because it tolerates doubt, it lives in doubt. This is its virtue, and its trap.

Every other creed shields itself with armour. Fascism silences dissent. Theocracy punishes blasphemy. Communism executes doubt as betrayal. Corporatism silences whistleblowers with NDAs. These ideologies appear stronger than they are because they never allow their foundations to be tested.

But liberalism? It permits criticism even of itself. And so, the dogpile begins. Citizens critique it to improve it, as they should. Wolves critique it to destroy it, as they always will. And the sound is indistinguishable. To the casual ear, it seems as if liberalism alone is illegitimate, while the wolves' creeds are too sacred or dangerous to question.

This is a lie. And it is killing us.

The sheepdog sees clearly: the ability to criticise liberalism is not proof of its weakness. It is proof of its strength. But critique is not an invitation to dismantle the walls while wolves circle the pasture. Before we indulge in tearing down, we must secure what stands. Before we question what makes us great, we must drive out those who would burn it down.

Critique is a tool for repair, not a licence for ruin. It sharpens institutions. It improves laws. It reminds leaders they are fallible. But when critique becomes a ritual of self-loathing, when it becomes the only voice in the square, it hollows the ground beneath our feet.

Liberalism must recover its balance: outward in defence, inward in reflection. First the wolves must be held at bay. Only then can the fences be mended, the pasture renewed.

For the allowance of critique was never meant as a gift to those who despise it. It was meant as a discipline for those who love it.

And enough is enough.

For when critique is mistaken for virtue in itself, it ceases to sharpen and begins to erode. What follows is not renewal, but drift. And drift, left untended, has only one destination: entropy.

The Entropy of Extremes

Liberalism's greatest danger is not only the wolves at the gate. It is the gravity within, the slow drift toward entropy.

Every society faces this pull. When balance weakens, extremes gather. When extremes clash, violence follows. This is not prophecy. It is nature.

Entropy is the law of neglect. It begins quietly, in the small failures of vigilance: laws unenforced, rules bent, trust ignored. At first, it looks like freedom. In time, it becomes collapse. For when order weakens, opportunists thrive. Where moderation falters, extremes grow fat. And once the middle is hollow, nothing remains to hold the field together.

This spiral is not a revolution. It is anti-revolution: not a leap forward but a collapse downward. It promises clarity, but brings chaos. It promises purity, but breeds vengeance. It promises safety, but delivers only blood.

Sheepdog Liberalism is the revolt against this collapse. A reverse revolution. Not the storming of palaces, but the rebuilding of fences. Not the purging of order, but the purging of wolves. It rejects the lie that freedom is weakness, or that balance is cowardice. It refuses to let liberty be mocked into silence or extremes be flattered into power.

Entropy is not inevitable. But it is relentless. Left unopposed, it will turn comfort into fragility, fragility into fear, and fear into violence. The sheepdog does not wait for that day. It stands early, holds firm, and remembers what is at stake.

Because when societies abandon balance, they do not drift into harmony. They entropy into chaos. And in chaos, the wolves always feast.

The Sheepdog's Call

To be British is to be liberal.

Not in the shallow, slogan-stamped sense of modern politics, but in the older, deeper sense.

In the belief that liberty is sacred. That law must serve the citizen, not rule them. That power, wherever it lives, must answer to justice.

And to be a Sheepdog Liberal is to be a patriot.

Not proud of symbols for their own sake, but proud to protect what they represent.

Fierce in duty. Unyielding in principle. Loyal not to blood, but to belief.

It is a call to arms, not of violence, but of vigilance.

A moral rallying cry, to stand between what we love and what seeks to tear it down.

Because the values we speak of – freedom, fairness, pluralism – are not made of steel.

They are fragile. Held together not by fate, but by generations willing to stand watch.

They demand courage to protect. Strength to preserve.

And guardians who will not blink when the wolves circle,

whether cloaked in flags, in faith, or in false compassion.

This is why Sheepdog Liberalism cannot be passive. It cannot be polite.

It does not wait quietly in committee rooms while the pillars of liberty decay.

It does not retreat when slandered by extremists.

It does not apologise for believing that Britain is worth defending.

Because to defend liberalism is to defend Britain itself.

And to protect Britain's future, we must be the sheepdog. Loyal not to a tribe of heritage, but to a tribe of values. Standing watch. Barking when needed. Biting when we must.

The wolves are real. And they are hungry.

If we do not defend this nation's soul, no one will.

The Values It Protects

Sheepdog Liberalism stands on the timeless foundations of classical liberalism, but it is not naive about what it takes to protect them.

What follows are not slogans. They are the pillars of a society worth defending:

- Freedom under law; not chaos under licence. Liberty is not the absence of rules. It is the presence of fairness; where justice is swift, laws are clear, and no one stands above them.

- Equality before the state; not submission to religion or ideology. In a liberal nation, your rights are not dictated by your faith, your politics, or your group identity. You are protected as an individual.

- Harmony through pluralism; not surrender to those who reject coexistence. We celebrate difference, but not at the cost of our shared civic fabric. There is no liberty in appeasing those who despise it.

- Protection of the individual; not just from the state, but from unchecked corporations, ideological coercion, and foreign interference. Power hides in many places. We confront them all.

And above all:

The state has a duty to its citizens. Not simply to manage them, but to protect their lives, their freedoms, and their future.

When that duty is ignored, when no one defends the shared rules, the shared space, or the shared truth, society begins to fracture.

That is when opportunists rise. That is when trust collapses. That is when tyranny finds its opening.

And that is when the wolves begin to gather.

This is what Sheepdog Liberalism exists to guard against.

Why Freedom Requires Strength

Freedom is not the default shape of human life.

Where people gather, they build hierarchies: ladders of strength, command, obedience. From small bands to great nations, power seeks a centre, and those who find it set the terms for everyone else. This is neither cynicism nor romance; it is the gravity of human order.

Freedom is not always attacked by armies. More often, it is chipped away – not with bullets, but with excuses, loopholes, and apathy. History demonstrates this, and our own century is proving it again: the wolves do not always roar at the gate, they slip inside quietly.

Liberalism does not abolish that gravity. It redirects it.

It says the centre of power shall be bound to law; that strength shall serve the citizen; that difference shall live unafraid inside the same field. But these are not self-keeping arrangements. If the liberal order refuses to carry strength within itself, a rival order will carry it against liberalism. Where a pasture shows no guardian, the wolves do not debate; they enter.

How the Wolves Enter

They do not always leap the fence. More often they find the unlatched gate.

Some enter by *infiltration*: they borrow the language of rights to unmake the rules that keep rights real.

Some enter by *extraction*: they graze without tending, fencing off common grass, poisoning streams, leaving the flock thinner and the field bare.

Some enter by *coercion*: they organise fear, cloak it in certainty, and teach the sheep to doubt the pasture itself.

These are not separate creatures but familiar behaviours of power. They exploit drift. When watchfulness softens into politeness, when boundaries fade into embarrassment, when law becomes theatre, the wolves learn the routes between the trees and the fold.

There is no virtue in letting your house burn down while you quote Voltaire.

Why Strength Is Necessary

If freedom is to endure, it must develop a spine.

Not to dominate, but to endure. Not to silence, but to prevent silencing.

Freedom has never survived on politeness alone. It survives only when someone is willing to bark and, if pressed, to bite.

The sheepdog exists for this exact reason: to convert the necessary fact of strength into a disciplined service of the field. Its bark is warning; its bite is boundary. It acts early so the pasture remains a place where sheep can graze together without fear.

This is the paradox liberalism must accept: a freedom that cannot act will not last. An order that will not enforce itself will be replaced by one that will. A field without a guardian does not remain open; it changes hands.

The Leash

Because strength can keep freedom, it must be kept by freedom.

The sheepdog's power is leashed to purpose; to the law that applies to all; to the limits that hold even in fear; to the duty that remembers what is being guarded. Where strength forgets its purpose, it ceases to be defence and becomes appetite. Strength must be bound twice, at the fence that keeps danger out, and at the leash that keeps duty in.

The lesson is simple and difficult: liberty that refuses strength will be ruled by it. The field remains free only when its guardian is willing and able to stand, and bound enough to stand for the right things.

To refuse strength is not kindness. It is consent to collapse.

Liberty that refuses strength consents to rule by the strong.

History shows this without exception: strength will govern; the only question is whether it serves freedom or devours it.

The Paradox of Power: Strength Without Surrender

Sheepdog Liberalism accepts a truth modern politics too often forgets: freedom cannot survive without the will to defend it.

But it also knows that defence without limits becomes domination.

Power without principle is tyranny. Principle without power is surrender.

The sheepdog stands between the two. Its teeth are real, but they are leashed. Its vigilance is fierce, but it always remembers what it is guarding.

The paradox is simple: strength must exist inside liberalism, or it will be claimed by its enemies. Yet strength must remain bound to law, or it will become the enemy itself.

Markets Without Morals Become Weapons

Markets are not natural. They are moral inventions.

They were built on trust, on contract, on fairness. A pasture fenced by law, where ambition could graze without devouring the field itself.

But fences weaken. When oversight fades and duty is forgotten, markets drift. They stop rewarding contribution and begin rewarding domination. They cease to be engines of opportunity and become engines of extraction.

A pasture without care is soon stripped bare. Fences rot, streams turn foul, the grass thins until even the flock itself begins to doubt the ground it stands on. Markets without mission devour the field they need to live.

Freedom cannot be sustained by appetite alone; without duty to tend the field, liberty itself withers.

The Consequence of Drift

The harm is not only economic; it is civic.

When markets forget their mission, the flock begins to weaken. Institutions of liberal order – courts, schools, parliaments, regulators – lose vigour. They appear inefficient, unjust, captured by appetite rather than guided by duty.

And when institutions falter, citizens withdraw their trust. They see unfairness where there should be balance, paralysis where there should be purpose. They lose confidence in the fences that hold, in the guardians that watch, in the pasture that sustains them.

No order can survive once its institutions are doubted more than they are believed.

When belief recedes, the pasture does not stand empty. It is seized. Rival powers rush in; some promising order, others purity, others fire. Each feeds on the despair left when fairness and efficiency are gone.

The Sheepdog's Duty

The sheepdog does not hate the pasture, nor those who graze upon it. It knows the field can flourish.

But it knows, too, that grazing must be guided. That the grass must be tended for tomorrow as well as today.

It stands watch not to curb ambition, but to stop exploitation. It defends not against growth, but against greed without limit. It draws the line where appetite forgets duty.

This is not anti-enterprise. It is pro-fairness.

The sheepdog does not close the field. It keeps it open by holding back those who would fence it off for themselves.

Liberalism must remember this: markets are not neutral. They are tools, and tools can be turned into weapons.

When they lose their mission, they corrode the very soil they depend on.

An untended market devours its own pasture, and a flock that no longer trusts the field will become easy prey for the wolves of chaos.

Democracy, a Gate Left Unlatched

Even democracy, the brightest pasture of liberal society, can be turned against itself.

Its rules can be bent into weapons. Its freedoms can be used to weaken freedom. Its openness can become a mask for those who seek not to share power, but to end it.

Liberalism makes its gravest mistake when it confuses tolerance with surrender.

We are told we must tolerate the intolerant.
We are told we must debate those who seek to end debate.
We are told that drawing lines is somehow illiberal.

That is not liberalism. It is surrender.

Democracy is not self-keeping. It cannot defend itself by ritual alone.

It survives only when guarded with strength, clarity, and conviction.

For the ballot box is not a toy to be played with by those who hate it.

It is the cornerstone of liberal order; and like every cornerstone, it must be defended or the whole house falls.

Democracy endures only when it is strong enough to resist those who would use it to destroy it.

The Sheep Forgot What They Were Defending, and the Wolves Sharpened Their Teeth

Liberalism must not confuse openness with obedience.

It must not treat democracy as if it must accommodate its own enemies.

- You do not let those who despise pluralism use pluralism to destroy.
- You do not give freedom to those who preach submission.
- You do not welcome the arsonist into the house simply because they asked politely.

Democracy is sacred. But it is not suicidal.

It must be defended with strength, clarity, and moral confidence.

The ballot box is not a weakness to be exploited by those who hate democracy.

It is the gate through which liberty enters, and it must never fall to the wolves.

Sheepdog Liberalism

Sheepdog Liberalism does not answer the threats of our time with nostalgia.

It answers with resolve.

Not with utopian dreams, but with real-world defences.

- We will not allow corporate monopolies to erode national life and public trust.
- We will not allow foreign-funded ideologues to exploit the freedoms they seek to dismantle.
- We will not allow wolves in sheep's clothing to vote liberalism out of existence.

Because freedom is not passive.

It must be watched. It must be guarded. And when necessary, it must be fought for.

It is better to bare teeth in defence of freedom than to kneel while it is crushed.

And this siege is not Britain's alone. Every free society faces it, or will, in time. The pasture may change, but the pattern does not. When trust in law and institutions thins, the wolves find their way in.

In a fertile valley nestled between ancient forests and gentle slopes stood a thriving pasture. Its grass was lush, its waters ran clear, and within it grazed a peaceful flock; not representing the people, but the precious legacy of liberal values, traditions, and institutions passed from generation to generation.

But prosperity breeds complacency. Gates once sturdy became rusted; fences strong enough to deter any intruder fell quietly into disrepair. Guardians, sheepdogs tasked to protect this liberal order, grew idle and slow, lulled into comfort by enduring peace. The flock itself, embodying institutions of tolerance, law, reason, and freedom, believed danger was a relic of the past, ignoring faint rustling at the forest's edge.

Yet beyond the tree line, hungry eyes watched, ever patient.

VOLUME II: The Siege

The Wolves Circle

The Sheepdog's Last Stand

Liberalism is under siege.

Not by one enemy, but many. Not by one idea, but by a pack of predators, circling in from every angle. Each has its own ideology, its own hunger, its own plan for the flock.

Some wear uniforms. Others wear smiles, hashtags, or robes.

They don't march in lines. They creep in through systems, movements, platforms, and pulpits. They call themselves saviours, reformers, revolutionaries, or realists; but they are wolves all the same.

Make no mistake: they do not want to debate liberalism. They want to bury it.

They want to replace your rights with obedience.

Your individuality with submission.

Your freedom with a flag, a scripture, a bloodline, or a corporate slogan.

They are the fascist strongman, the Islamist theocrat, the radical accelerationist, the resentful puritan of the far left, and the profit-choked monopolist who would sell your soul for a dividend.

Each believes they are the answer to a broken world. Each believes their truth should reign, even if it means silencing yours.

And while they fight for domination, there are too few fighting for liberalism. Not the hollow liberalism of hashtags and empty gestures, but real liberalism: rule of law, pluralism, civic equality, and freedom with responsibility.

That is why the sheepdog must stand.
Because when the wolves circle, someone must bark.
When they leap, someone must bite.
Sheepdog Liberalism does not stand for empire or utopia.

It stands for the ordinary citizen. For the shopkeeper, the teacher, the mother, the neighbour. Those who want to live freely, speak freely, believe freely, and raise their children in peace.

But today's liberalism does not defend itself.
It needs defenders. It needs teeth.
It needs courage.

Because if liberalism falls to any one of these wolves, the whole flock goes with it.

This is the final warning. This is the final call.
The sheepdog does not wait for permission.
It stands, or there is nothing left to stand for.

The wolves did not come roaring and snarling. They came gently, each disguised, slipping through the rusted gates and weakened fences unnoticed, each bringing their unique devastation.

***

The Red Wolf: Eating Its Own Den

The wolf in sheep's clothing does not snarl. It speaks softly of fairness, justice, and kindness. It tells the flock it comes not to harm, but to help. To share the pasture more equally.

But beneath the fleece is a predator. One that does not guard against the wolves, but opens the gates for them. One that, after letting the wolves in, turns and devours its own.

This is the Red Wolf, the predator born of the radical left. It claims to be an agent of progress, but its foundation is not compassion; it is envy. Not responsibility, but control. Not healing, but destruction.

Revolution's Broken Promises

Revolutionary movements have long promised justice. But too often, they have delivered cages.

In the French Revolution, the cry for liberty led to the Reign of Terror. The guillotine did not stop with kings. It turned inward, killing those deemed impure by the new regime.

In Russia, 1917 promised equality. By 1937, Stalin's purges had executed hundreds of thousands of party loyalists, including the very architects of the revolution.

In Cambodia, the Khmer Rouge promised to liberate peasants from elite control. Instead, they murdered intellectuals for wearing glasses.

Each time, the pattern is the same. Utopian dreams spiral into authoritarian nightmares. The state becomes the ideology. The ideology becomes a weapon, used not just against enemies, but against dissenters, moderates, and eventually, its own children.

And always, liberalism is the first thing to die.

Free speech is erased.

The rule of law is replaced by decree.

The individual is dissolved into a collective, defined by the loudest or most ruthless voices in the room.

***

A New Language, The Same Intolerance

In our time, the far left has largely abandoned revolutionary violence, but not revolutionary thinking. The weapons have changed. Instead of bullets, it now wields purges of reputation. Instead of exile, it uses social shunning. Instead of trials, it holds tribunals on timelines.

Its targets are not always the powerful. Often, they are the nearly-aligned. Those close enough to care, but too independent to conform.

A feminist who questions orthodoxy.
A gay man who critiques gender theory.
A minority business owner who believes in capitalism.

Each is framed as a traitor. Not for causing harm, but for failing to repeat the latest slogan with perfect timing and tone.

This is not pluralism. It is a secular inquisition.

Liberalism creates space for disagreement. The far left seeks to erase it. It speaks of solidarity, but it enforces conformity. It claims to build, but its instinct is to destroy. The progressive wolf does not build. It purges. It eats its own den. It turns on its allies, devours nuance, and replaces solidarity with shame. And in doing so, it hollows out the very communities it claims to defend.

When the Left Turned Inward: A British Lesson

Britain has seen this unfold in full view.

Under Jeremy Corbyn's leadership, the Labour Party, once a coalition of workers, reformers, and civic-minded social democrats, fell under the sway of a hard-left vanguard. One more interested in ideological alignment than public trust.

The antisemitism crisis was not an outlier. It was a symptom. Behind it was a culture of litmus tests, loyalty oaths, and purges.

MPs were deselected over tone. Feminists were harassed for questioning doctrine. Pro-enterprise policies were equated with betrayal. To stay in the movement, one had to conform not only in belief, but in posture, language, and ritual.

The result was a party obsessed with internal purity, disconnected from the communities it claimed to represent.

Labour's vote collapsed across the working-class North and Midlands not because voters rejected justice, but because they no longer recognised those claiming to speak for it.

What began as a movement for fairness became a performance of righteousness. And the wolves, sensing the vacuum, circled.

False Virtue, Real Fragility

The left-wing wolf does not build institutions, it dismantles them. It claims to stand for the marginalised, but often speaks only for its own self-image. It proposes economic collapse as liberation, yet offers no replacement for stability, infrastructure, or civic trust.

In place of contribution, it offers condemnation.
In place of innovation, it offers entitlement.
In place of policy, it offers performance.

It promises a post-ownership, post-labour, post-state future, but cannot describe how food will be grown, roads maintained, or security kept. It tears down with ease and calls the ruins justice.

Sheepdog Liberalism does not oppose idealism. It believes in reform. It believes inequality, corruption, and exclusion are real. But it does not believe in chaos as a cure. It holds billionaires accountable with regulation and tax, not mobs and guillotines. It supports fairness, not forced uniformity.

We fix what is broken. We do not burn what still stands.

What the Far Left Forgets

The most painful irony is this: liberalism made the dreams of progressives possible. It was liberalism that abolished slavery, that ended child labour, that secured voting rights and decriminalised homosexuality. It was liberal societies, not utopian ones, that gave space for marginalised voices to rise.

The far left seeks to dismantle the very framework that allowed it to speak.

And so, the sheepdog must stand. Not to silence critics, but to guard the space where critique remains free. Not to block change, but to protect the foundation upon which lasting change is possible.

Because when liberalism falls, from the left or the right, the silence that follows does not discriminate.

It swallows everyone.

He arrived softly, in sheep's clothing, speaking words of fairness and compassion. He told the sheepdog that barking was violence, that fences oppressed, that vigilance was paranoia. Some sheep applauded him, wandering far from the protection of the dog and the herd, dismantling fences, calling their guardian a tyrant. The Red Wolf left behind a flock divided and lost, mistrusting each other and their protector.

The Fascist Wolf: The False Saviour at the Gate

Some wolves do not hide. They do not wear a fleece or speak softly. They stand at the gate, loud and proud, promising to restore what was lost.

The fascist wolf does not pretend to be a sheep. He tells the sheep they are weak, that their protectors are liars, and that only he can save them. He wraps himself in the flag, not out of patriotism, but as a symbol of dominance. He does not fight for freedom. He fights to own it.

He names enemies, not solutions. The foreigner. The dissenter. The outsider. He speaks not with compassion, but with certainty.

"You are suffering," he says, "because of them."

This is not strength. It is seduction. The promise of safety, in exchange for submission.

When the Saviour Becomes the Tyrant

Fascism rarely begins with violence. It begins with humiliation, national shame, and the longing for clarity. It speaks to a people who feel betrayed and abandoned. Then it offers simplicity. A mythologised past. An invented purity. A single strong hand to restore it all.

The flock does not turn to the wolf without reason. It turns when the sheepdogs grow complacent, or when the fences of trust begin to rot. When parties grow stale, corrupt, or detached, citizens no longer believe the field is tended. Into that emptiness steps the populist. He does not begin with chains or camps, but with promises; jobs restored, borders defended, pride renewed. At first it feels like renewal. But each promise demands more power, fewer checks, less room for dissent. And step by step, the saviour leads the flock closer to the cage.

In Italy, Mussolini did not rise through tanks. He marched with veterans, wore polished uniforms, and promised dignity. He offered a fantasy of rebirth. But once in power, he gutted the courts, crushed dissent, and turned the press into a mouthpiece for the state. Order became obedience. Dignity became fear.

In Germany, Hitler was not elected by monsters. He was elected by citizens exhausted by inflation, demoralised by defeat, and disillusioned with their leaders. He told them they were not to blame. He pointed outward. The Jews. The communists. The elites. The result was the Holocaust. Not an aberration, but a consequence of the logic he had seeded from the start.

The British Variant

In recent years, movements that once lived on the margins have stepped into the public square. The far right no longer whispers online. It organises rallies, promotes candidates, and captures airtime. Parties like Reform capitalise on public frustration – not to serve it, but to inflame it.

They are right about some symptoms. Trust is eroding. The pace of immigration, without adequate planning or integration, has strained communities. Too many institutions speak past the people they claim to represent.

But their answer is not reform. It is retreat. Close the gates. Blame the outsider. Flatten complexity into tribal slogans.

And beneath it all lies a deeper weakness: they have no philosophy. No structure to hold them steady. One day they rage against elites, the next they praise them. One week they call for liberty, the next they cheer for bans. To hand power to such a movement is to roll dice with the nation's future at stake, never knowing what hand will be played next.

Worse, their energy feeds on escalation. What begins as grievance soon turns to scapegoating. What begins as frustration curdles into resentment, then into racial hatred and division. Their path does not renew a nation. It corrodes it.

They saw the chaos and offered clarity. They saw the apathy and offered energy. They saw a frightened public and offered the illusion of safety, at the cost of freedom.

This is not a plan for renewal. It is a plan for collapse.

Knowsley: When the Mask Slips

In Knowsley, outside a hotel housing asylum seekers, far right agitators incited a mob. Police vans were torched. Officers were pelted with bricks and fireworks. Rumours – some true, many false – were weaponised into rage.

Among them were stories of grooming gangs, real scandals where the state failed victims. But the fascist wolf does not seek justice. He seeks vengeance. He does not distinguish the criminal from the refugee. He does not want resolution. He wants reaction.

What began as pain was turned into panic. Not through policy. Through performance.

A riot, not a remedy.

This was not a protest. It was a theatre. And a warning.

The fascist wolf had arrived not through a manifesto, but via a riot. Not through Parliament, but via panic.

And after the smoke cleared, what followed?

Not accountability. Not solutions.
Silence.

No serious crackdown on the networks behind it. No systemic response to the lies spread online. No moral line drawn by national leadership.

On the ground, it was the community, not the agitators, who returned to clean the streets, repair the damage, and help each other recover. That is the true face of Britain: ordinary people refusing to let chaos define them.

Yet the cost remained. Burned-out vans, shattered windows, and public money drained into repairs instead of schools, hospitals, or housing. The riots did not defend Britain. They weakened it.

And that silence from above, combined with the wreckage below, is what the fascist feeds on. If no one pushes back, he learns just how far the line can be moved – until there is no line left at all.

The Myth of Strength

Fascism speaks of strength, but it delivers only domination. It replaces justice with decree, unity with obedience, and freedom with fear. It says it will restore order, but it does so by dismantling the institutions that hold a society together.

In Hungary, Viktor Orbán won power through elections. Then he rewrote the system that allowed those elections to matter. Courts were hollowed. Journalists threatened. Civic space narrowed. Democracy existed in name, but not in function.

Even in Britain the ground has been tested. In 2019, a Prime Minister attempted to suspend Parliament for weeks during the height of a national crisis. The courts struck it down, but the attempt revealed how fragile our safeguards can be when power decides scrutiny is an obstacle. It was not a coup, nor a dictatorship, but it showed how easily technicalities can be used to stretch the limits of constitutional order. Strong guardrails matter, because once they bend, they invite further pressure.

In the United States, Donald Trump now prepares for a second term with a loyalist blueprint to reshape the civil service, sideline independent agencies, and assert personal control over the machinery of government. His "Project 2025" is not a platform. It is a warning. A free society, redesigned to serve one man.

We have seen where this path leads. Every time, the tragedy ends the same. Institutions rot. Neighbours divide. The nation becomes a reflection of the leader's ego, and nothing more.

Fascism Finds Openings

Fascism does not rise because people dream of tyranny. It rises when liberalism forgets to defend itself. When institutions drift into abstraction. When communities feel unheard. When leaders confuse symbolic gestures for service.

And into that vacuum steps the fascist. Not because he is persuasive, but because he is present. He offers answers before liberalism finds its voice.

The sheepdog does not deny that people are angry. It does not pretend the system is flawless. But it refuses to let pain be weaponised into prejudice.

It does not meet chaos with submission. It meets it with a barrier. Strong laws. Honest leadership. Unflinching clarity about who we are and what we stand for.

True Patriotism Barks First

True patriotism is not nostalgia. It is not exclusion. It is not silence while the walls are dismantled in the name of strength.

It is the quiet courage to protect what is real, not what is romanticised. To draw the line early, before the damage spreads. To say: you may be angry, but you do not get to burn it down.

The sheepdog does not retreat. It does not chase purity. It stands between chaos and community. Between propaganda and principle.

It guards the gate not just from foreign threats, but from the fantasy of purity that has destroyed so many nations from within.

Because fascism never starts with boots. It begins with excuses.

And if we are too polite to name it, we will be too late to stop it.

When disorder grew, a strong and confident voice called from the gate, promising security and clarity. He blamed outsiders and dissenters, sowing suspicion. He convinced the sheep that their fatness made them vulnerable, that strength came only through purity. Sheep turned on sheep, trusting strength rather than wisdom, and peace became fear. The fascist wolf left a field scarred by paranoia and violence.

The Islamist Wolf: The Patient Predator at the Gate

The theocratic wolf has many faces. Once, it wore the crown of popes and the robes of inquisitors. It burned scientists in the name of scripture, silenced dissent with holy fire, and demanded obedience not to the law of man, but to the voice of God, as interpreted by men who sought power more than peace.

In Britain today, that wolf has changed its coat, but not its nature. Its modern form is Islamism. Not Islam, but Islamism. A political movement cloaked in religious garb, that seeks not to live within liberal society, but to replace it.

This distinction matters. **The Muslim is not the wolf. The Islamist is.**

The peaceful British Muslim is no less a citizen than the peaceful British Christian or Jew. But the Islamist is no less an enemy than the fascist or the communist. His aim is not prayer, but power: the slow conquest of institutions, culture, and law. He does not charge the gates. He enters quietly, then whispers that the walls are unjust, the sheepdog oppressive, the liberal order itself sinful and obsolete.

This is not paranoia. It is history.

The Long Siege: What Islamism Looks Like

Islamism is not just a religion, it is a political blueprint. Its sacred texts are not confined to personal ethics; they include laws of conquest, punishment, and governance. It offers not just a way to live, but a way to rule, and that rule is not liberal.

Look to the past: the conquest of North Africa and the Middle East, where diverse societies – pagan, Jewish, Christian, animist – were absorbed or erased. The Arabization and Islamization of vast lands was not a peaceful integration but a dominance of one truth over many. Languages vanished. Traditions died. Coexistence ended.

Or look to Iran. A country that once stood at the edge of modernity. Before 1979, Iran had television, secular universities, cinema, fashion. Women studied freely, and pluralism, while imperfect, existed. But then the Islamists took power. Today, women are murdered for refusing the hijab, gays are executed in public squares, and dissent is crushed by morality police. It is not faith. It is tyranny draped in scripture.

Britain is not Iran. But Islamism plays a long game. It does not need guns when it has guilt. It does not need violence when it has influence.

It whispers into the ears of liberals:

"You are racist if you speak against us."

"You are Islamophobic if you question our preachers."

"You must accommodate our ways, even when we reject yours."

And while the sheep stumble over politeness, the wolf plants its seeds in schools, mosques, universities, and foreign-funded think tanks. It is not integration. It is infiltration.

When We Fail to Act, Fascism Responds

History tells us what happens when the Islamist wolf is left to grow unchecked: eventually, the fascist wolf will come. and he will not distinguish between friend and foe.

It happened in Spain, when the Reconquista expelled Muslims and Jews alike, after centuries of Islamic rule. In the name of defending Christendom, Catholic monarchs purged entire populations, punishing not only oppressors but peaceful communities who had long coexisted. We see similar patterns today in France, where legitimate concerns about Islamist separatism and terror attacks have led to sweeping crackdowns, not just on radicals, but on the broader Muslim population. Mosques shuttered. Civil liberties curtailed. And in India, Hindu nationalism has risen sharply in response to decades of Islamist violence in Kashmir and elsewhere, and now targets peaceful Muslims indiscriminately. The cycle repeats: when liberalism fails to enforce its own values clearly and early, the pendulum swings not toward justice, but vengeance.

When Islamist extremism grows, it provokes a backlash. And that backlash does not ask for nuance. It doesn't care if you are a peaceful Muslim or a radical one. It targets the headscarf and the skin tone, not the ideology. And it brings with it a flood of new victims: Jews, Sikhs, Hindus, liberals, the poor, the different.

The Sheepdog Liberal does not wait for this to unfold. He draws the line before it escalates. He defends the mosque from the fascist, and the mosque from the Islamist. He guards the school not only from far right indoctrination, but from Salafist or Qatari propaganda. He defends the right to worship, but not the right to preach hatred.

He knows this isn't just about national security. It's about civic survival.

Liberalism Must Draw Boundaries, Or Be Replaced

Stopping the Islamist wolf requires more than platitudes about tolerance or vague hopes for "integration." It demands action grounded not in paranoia, but in clarity. A liberal society cannot afford to be naive about threats that wear the cloak of faith while undermining the very freedom that allows them to exist.

We must draw the line clearly, firmly, and unapologetically.

That means rooting out Islamist ideology wherever it festers: in schools, mosques, charities, and online platforms, especially when funded or influenced by regimes that despise our freedoms. It means cutting off Qatari and other authoritarian money that quietly flows into universities and cultural institutions, reshaping the minds of young people under the guise of "education."

It means enforcing not just laws, but values. You are free to believe in God. You are not free to call for the downfall of liberal democracy from the pulpit. You are free to fast, to pray, to wear what your faith demands. You are not free to preach that women are inferior, or that apostates deserve death, or that your God's law replaces Britain's. That is the line. Faith is a private right, not a political sword.

It means every new citizen must understand: you are not entering a void. You are joining a covenant. A civic contract. You are free to be Muslim, Christian, Sikh, or atheist, but only so long as you also believe in equality, free speech, and the rule of law. If you want to enjoy liberalism, you must help defend it.

This will take education. It will take transparency in our institutions. It will take investment in communities before extremists get to them. And yes, it will take difficult conversations. But it must be done. Because the alternative is always the same: a liberal state that refuses to act creates a vacuum, and into that vacuum steps the fascist wolf.

Liberalism is not kept alive by wishful thinking. It is kept alive by courage.

The Sheepdog Barks for All

To some, this may seem harsh. But the harshest truth is this:

If liberalism refuses to defend itself, it will not survive.

And when it dies, it is not just the secular who will suffer, it is also the faithful.

The Muslim who believes in democracy, who loves this country, who teaches his daughter that she may choose her own life. *He* will be one of the first crushed under the Islamist regime. Just as Jews were crushed under Catholic monarchs. Just as Protestants were burned by Catholic kings. Just as atheists are hunted by mullahs today.

The sheepdog does not hate religion. He honours freedom of worship. He will protect the synagogue, the church, the mosque – but not if they house wolves.

He is not silent out of politeness. He is not blind out of fear. He draws the line. clearly, calmly, early.

Because once the Islamist wolf is inside the walls, it is not the sheepdog he kills first.

It is the sheep who trusted him.

Observing patiently, the Islamist wolf waited at the broken fence, gentle in voice, insisting that his intentions were pure. He convinced some sheep to invite him in, whispering of community and certainty. Once within the pasture he quietly set fires to the field, burning the very grass that nourished the flock, leaving only barren ground and confusion in his wake.

The Corporate Wolf: The Predator in a Suit

Not every wolf growls. Some wear tailored suits. Some shake hands. Some sponsor the evening news.

The corporate wolf does not rant or preach. It smiles and optimises, promising growth while bleeding a nation dry.

It does not attack liberalism head-on. It feeds on its excess. It thrives not when freedom is defended, but when it is unguarded. Where regulation is weak, oversight timid, and public trust exhausted, the corporate wolf quietly sharpens its teeth.

This wolf does not speak of ideology. It speaks of efficiency. It does not campaign to rule. It lobbies to be exempt. It wants your freedom, not to destroy it, but to sell it back to you in monthly instalments.

The Rise of the Market Without a Compass

Liberalism built the free market. It recognised that enterprise, when matched with rules, fuels innovation, prosperity, and choice.

Corporations are not villains by design. At their best they are engines of prosperity; building wealth for families, creating jobs for communities, and fuelling the innovation that lifts entire nations. They are one of the bedrocks of modern liberal societies, proof that enterprise can turn ambition into abundance. But like all wolves, when the leash is loosed and the rules ignored, what begins as wealth-building turns into hoarding. What begins as efficiency turns into exploitation. And what began as growth for the many becomes extraction for the few. Enterprise builds nations, but when it drifts unrestrained, it begins to consume them.

But when liberalism forgets to enforce its own guardrails, markets do not stay free. They become rigged. They reward dominance, not value. They replace competition with consolidation. They extract, addict, and externalise cost onto the public.

This is how the corporate wolf was born. Not in a revolution, but in an era of drift. When citizens became consumers, and institutions began to ask not what serves the public, but what boosts the quarter.

This wolf whispers that exploitation is innovation.
That convenience is worth your sovereignty.

That your data is theirs to sell, your time theirs to monetise, your outrage theirs to weaponise.

It smiles while it steals.

And when no one stops it, it builds the gate that lets the other wolves in.

A Catalogue of Quiet Predation

Look at Britain.

Thames Water dumps sewage into public rivers while paying out billions in dividends to private investors. It claims its hands are tied, while its profits flow freely.

Amazon centralises commerce, undermines local shops, and pays next to nothing in taxes. Its convenience comes at the cost of entire high streets.

Betting companies target the poor with addictive algorithms. Their profits rise with each life wrecked. They sponsor sports teams while evading scrutiny and accountability.

BlackRock, and funds like it, treat housing not as a human need, but as an asset class. They buy up homes to sit on them, inflate their value, and bleed communities dry.

And when disaster strikes, the consequences are not abstract. At Grenfell Tower, cost-cutting killed. Corners were shaved by contractors, regulations overlooked, safety ignored. And still, no one was held accountable.

These are not random abuses. They are symptoms of a system where rules softened, institutions looked away, and profit became untouchable.

Freedom Cannot Be Rented Back

The danger of the corporate wolf is not only economic. It is political. It erodes the social contract. It hollows out trust in institutions. It leaves the citizen feeling powerless, watched, mined, and manipulated.

And when that trust dies, the door swings open for the others.

The far right demagogue points to the decay and says, "Tear it down."
The accelerationist whispers, "Let it all burn."
The theocrat says, "This is what godlessness brings."

But it was not freedom that failed. It was the refusal to defend it.

If liberalism stands for anything, it must stand for rules that bind even the powerful. A government that answers not to donors, but to the people. A market that serves communities, not cannibalises them.

Not Anti-Business. Anti-Corruption

This is not a rejection of capitalism. It is a defence of real enterprise.

Liberalism believes in the power of trade, innovation, and private ambition. It believes that a shopkeeper building a business, a founder launching a company, or a worker turning their skill into income should be protected and empowered.

But none of that is possible when monopolies rig the game, when corruption replaces fairness, and when red tape chokes the small while the giant walks free.

Breaking up monopolies is not anti-business. It is pro-competition.

Taxing loopholes is not anti-growth. It is how we fund the ground businesses stand on.

Protecting consumers is not interference. It is the price of legitimacy.

A liberal market is one where the builder, the innovator, and the honest player can win, not just those with the best lawyers and the biggest lobbyists.

The Wolf in Many Disguises

The corporate wolf does not tear down the gate. It buys the land around it and supplies the cheapest wood for the gate. It whispers that loyalty is for fools, that regulation is red tape, and that civic duty is a cost to be cut.

The despair it causes creates the vacuum in which fascism thrives.

The inequality it breeds becomes the rallying cry of the far left wolf.

The alienation it spreads leaves communities open to Islamist radicalism.

And worse, this wolf wears many faces.

It courts the left with slogans of inclusion, while exploiting the workers it claims to protect.

It flatters the right with talk of entrepreneurial freedom, while dodging the taxes that build roads, schools, and hospitals.

It donates to both sides. It lobbies every aisle. It wins by exhaustion.

It does not care which ideology wins.
Only that no one stops the bleeding.
This is not business. This is capture.
This is not capitalism. It is corrosion.
The wolves do not always storm the gates.
Sometimes they pay off the guards.

And that, too, is something worth biting over.

This wolf didn't snarl. He wore fine clothing and spoke of prosperity. He weakened gates by neglect, convincing sheep to sell their fences for profits, extracting trust for dividends. His presence eroded confidence and weakened defences, leaving sheep reliant on him alone, uncertain how to survive without his hollow generosity.

The Accelerationist Wolf: The Pyromaniac of Collapse

Some wolves want to rule. Others want to purify. This one simply wants to break the lock and see what happens next.

The accelerationist believes that society cannot be saved, only sped toward its breaking point so that something new can rise from the ashes.

The accelerationist wolf does not come with manifestos or scripture. It carries no blueprint. No endgame. It arrives wrapped in irony and detachment. It shrugs at every tradition, mocks every principle, and celebrates one thing above all: collapse.

It is not an ideologue; it is a saboteur. It does not want power; it wants the absence of order.

Where the fascist promises control, the accelerationist offers chaos.

Where the theocrat claims certainty, the accelerationist delights in confusion.

Where the corporatist consolidates, the accelerationist dissolves.

To this wolf, structure is oppression. Process is cowardice. And reform is weakness.

It sneers at the slow work of liberal democracy. It does not believe in building, only in breaking. Not because something better will rise, but because it wants to watch what falls.

But even the fire that set the field ablaze was first lit for warmth.

Accelerationists are not born from nothing. They rise from real grievances: from wealth piled at the top while wages stagnate below, from institutions that protect the powerful while failing the vulnerable, from a sense that the very system meant to guard justice has become its perpetrator. At first this impulse is not destructive. It is the same scepticism of power that built constitutions, demanded restraint, and reminded rulers that government must answer to the governed. But left unmoored, this instinct warps. Restraint becomes rejection. Critique becomes contempt. Inequality convinces them that reform is impossible, and so only collapse will do. What began as a call for limits mutates into a call for ruin. The accelerationist wolf does not prune the tree. He sets the field alight.

The Historical Warning: What Comes After the Fall

This is not new. History is littered with revolutionaries who promised emancipation through destruction, only to deliver tyranny.

In Russia, the Bolsheviks and revolutionary allies dismantled centuries of monarchy and hierarchy. But what came next was not freedom. It was famine, the Red Terror, gulags, secret police, and a paranoia so deep it consumed its own.

In China, Mao's Cultural Revolution was not a reformation. It was a purge. Youths were encouraged to denounce their elders. Books were burned. Teachers were beaten. Traditions were torn down. What followed was misery, surveillance, and silence.

In Germany, after Versailles, the Freikorps and early fascist movements sought to raze the republic and return pride through violence. Their collapse of consensus paved the way for Hitler.

In every case, the promise was transformation. The result was terror.

Collapse does not create renewal. It creates a vacuum.

And into that vacuum, power always rushes: brutal, hungry, and unopposed.

Revolution is not sexy. It is suffering. It is easy to romanticise collapse when you have never lived through it. The fetish for ruin belongs to those untouched by it, spectators who mistake other people's pain for purity. The accelerationist dreams of fire but forgets that he too can burn.

The Modern Form: Chaos with Wi-Fi

Today's accelerationist is not reading Marx in the shadows. He is streaming mayhem on social media. He is posting memes, inciting rage, and calling for collapse. Not from ideology, but from alienation.

He may call himself revolutionary, or based, or blackpilled. He might wear a hammer-and-sickle or wave a flag of chaos. But his belief system is hollow. He doesn't want to rebuild society. He wants it to end.

In 2011, riots swept across British cities. Sparked by injustice, hijacked by opportunism. No platform. No demand. Just fire, looting, and spectacle.

In online spaces, the same virus spreads. Threads, streams, and algorithms reward provocation over purpose. Doxxing, disruption, and digital arson become currencies of clout. There is no shared truth, only distortion and dopamine.

Accelerationism thrives here. It doesn't organise. It metastasises.

And as institutions fail to respond, the disillusioned gather. Not around solutions, but around the thrill of disorder.

***

Why Liberalism Struggles to Respond

Liberalism believes in process: in dialogue, rules, and restraint. It is designed to absorb disagreement and evolve through deliberation.

But accelerationism mocks all of that. It does not seek representation. It exploits openness to destroy the very space that allows dissent. It throws bricks, then livestreams the applause.

Liberalism, in its hesitation, tries to reason with the arsonist. It calls for empathy, platforms the provocateur, and hopes that radicalism will cool when understood.

But collapse does not debate. It only accelerates.

And every time liberalism hesitates to defend itself, accelerationism spreads further. Not because it is persuasive, but because it is loud, unfiltered, and endlessly replicated by machines.

This wolf does not wait for votes. It rides the algorithm.

Not a Movement, A Mood

This wolf is not united by belief. It is united by feeling: disgust at hypocrisy, contempt for authority, boredom with moderation, and a desire to see it all fall.

And in that vacuum of purpose, it becomes a gateway.

It does not care who walks through the ruins; a fascist, a theocrat, a strongman; as long as it is not the liberal. It will welcome the tyrant, if only to watch the system burn.

This is what makes the accelerationist wolf so dangerous. It does not want to rule. And that makes it easier to ignore, until it clears the way for someone who does.

What the Sheepdog Must Defend

The sheepdog cannot chase this wolf in the usual way. There is no platform to expose. No ideology to debate.

What must be defended is meaning itself: institutions, process, the shared space. Not because they are perfect, but because they are better than the void.

Liberalism must reclaim seriousness. It must stop mistaking irony for insight. It must call out destruction, even when wrapped in protest slogans or digital aesthetics.

This does not mean silencing dissent. It means confronting the lie that collapse is cleansing, that nothing matters, and that freedom is found in fire.

Because if nothing matters, anything becomes permissible. And when anything is permissible, power always wins.

Conclusion: The Fire Is Not a Phase

The accelerationist wolf may laugh at politics, but it plays a deadly game.

Its chaos clears the ground for authoritarians. Its cynicism corrodes trust. Its spectacle invites predators. It does not end systems. It weakens them, until the next wolf enters through the rubble.

Liberalism must understand: not all threats wear ideology.

Some wear jokes.
Some wear avatars.
Some wear apathy.

And that is no less dangerous than any other wolf at the gate.

Because if you wait until the fire touches your door, it is already too late to ask what the match was for.

Finally, a wolf came that didn't bother to disguise itself at all. He laughed at their confusion, encouraged chaos, and whispered that destruction was liberation. He set fires and kicked down fences for amusement, not caring what replaced the order, only delighting in its collapse. His arrival spread nihilism and despair, leaving sheep hopeless, scattered, and vulnerable.

Conclusion: Why Liberalism Needs Teeth

Liberalism was never supposed to be easy.

It demands more than slogans. It requires discipline: of thought, of tolerance, of restraint. It asks a public not just to vote, but to govern itself with dignity. To disagree without violence. To live in difference without division.

That strength has also made it fragile. Because liberalism assumes its own decency will be enough.

It isn't.

History does not protect what we fail to defend. And today, liberal societies are relearning an old truth: that tolerance without limits becomes surrender, and openness without vigilance invites collapse.

The threats we face are not accidental. They are exaggerations of the very values we need.

Enterprise; left unmoored, becomes exploitation: the corporate wolf.
Justice; unbalanced, becomes vengeance: the progressive wolf.
Faith; untempered, becomes domination: the theocratic wolf.
Pride; humiliated, becomes tyranny: the fascist wolf.
Restraint; unmoored from trust, becomes destruction: the accelerationist wolf.

None of these began as monsters. Each began as a reasonable human impulse; ambition, fairness, dignity, belonging. Each became dangerous when it demanded purity instead of balance, obedience instead of freedom.

And none of this is new. History is a graveyard of societies that forgot where the line lies. Weimar collapsed under humiliation. Rome hollowed itself through corruption. Revolutions in Russia, China, and beyond promised liberation but delivered terror. The wolves always return.

That is why the sheepdog matters. It is not an oppressor, but a guardian. It does not hunt enterprise, justice, faith, pride, or restraint, it keeps them from mutating into predators. It does not silence, but it sets boundaries. It does not extinguish ideals, but it keeps them tethered to the values that make Britain free: fairness, dignity, pluralism, law.

We are not under siege from a single enemy. We are surrounded by opportunists. Authoritarians. Theocrats. Demagogues. Accelerationists. They test the fences we stopped maintaining. They do not knock at the front door. They borrow our words – freedom, justice, inclusion – and use them to unmake the society that gave them meaning.

Liberalism, unsure of itself, too often retreats in the name of politeness. It allows the line to be redrawn, hoping things will stabilise on their own. They will not.

If liberalism is to endure, it must remember what gave it strength: not just its ideas, but its courage. Not just its freedoms, but its defences. We need a liberalism that does not apologise for existing. That draws lines with clarity. That refuses to tolerate those who exploit the openness they despise.

This is not a call to abandon liberty. It is a call to protect it with law, structure, and moral confidence.

Sheepdog Liberalism does not seek vengeance. It does not crave control. But it understands what liberalism has forgotten: that without guardians, freedom is just a memory waiting to fade.

Because not every threat wears a uniform.
Some speak in the language of rights.
Some march under the banner of justice.
Some dress their hunger for power in the robes of progress.
We must learn to tell the difference.
The wolves are already inside.

And if we are to keep this fragile, hard-won way of life, then liberalism must relearn how to bare its teeth. Not with anger. Not with fear.

But with duty.

The price of liberty is eternal vigilance. The sheepdog must never sleep.

The wolves are at the gate. But the sheepdog is not defenceless. He has teeth to meet them.

The 10 Teeth of the Sheepdog

At last, seeing the desolation, a lone sheepdog stepped forward. He had grown slow, unsteady from years of idleness, but he still bore teeth; the lessons forged from wisdom, resilience, and necessity. He understood now that the sheep – liberal institutions and ideals – were fragile things needing constant, careful defence. He had no choice but to act.

Yet the sheepdog faced resistance, hesitation, and even confusion from the endangered sheep he sought to protect. Each tooth was tested, hard-won, and painfully necessary.

Tooth 1: Order, the First Defence

Authoritarianism is not the exception. It is the norm. Across history, human beings have lived not in freedom, but under domination: emperors, warlords, cults, or kings. Rights were not expected. Law was not protection; it was power.

Liberalism is not humanity's natural state. It is its rebellion; a brief and fragile arrangement in which the individual is protected, law is impartial, and institutions serve the public rather than control it. It is an achievement, not an inevitability. Like all rare achievements, it survives only through vigilance.

Imagine a city in which the laws still exist, but they are no longer enforced. Where theft becomes common not because poverty rises, but because consequences vanish. Where street protests begin in genuine outrage but end in shattered glass. Where schools teach rights, but never responsibilities. Where parents no longer model discipline because the state no longer asks it of them.

In this city, the idea of freedom still exists in language, but not in practice. Speech becomes noise. Law becomes negotiation. Power shifts, not to principle, but to whoever can shout the loudest. Over time, the citizen learns not to trust the law, but to fear its absence. They do not feel liberated. They feel abandoned.

And here the wolves thrive. For nothing serves them better than a field without fences. They slip in under the cover of freedom, but what they deliver is only domination. Order is the tooth that keeps them out: the fence they cannot cross, the bite they cannot ignore.

And when fear replaces structure, people no longer ask who is right. They ask who is in charge.

Modern liberalism has forgotten this. It assumes that if we dismantle oppression, tolerance will blossom. That reason alone can out-argue zealotry. That decency is the default. But societies do not drift toward justice. They collapse toward entropy. And where structure fails, predators emerge. They do not arrive in tanks with guns. They arrive in hashtags, in ideologies, in soft voices that apologise for disorder. They promise freedom, but deliver only fire.

We have seen this before. In Weimar Germany, liberty existed on paper. Rights were abundant. But the republic lacked order and was plagued by inflation, ideological street violence, and institutional paralysis. The courts were weak. Political parties fought in the streets. Public authority collapsed. Into that vacuum stepped a man who promised not freedom, but order. First in slogans, then in uniforms. Hitler did not overthrow the system. He was invited in by its weakness.

Contrast that with South Korea in the decades after war and occupation. Its journey to democracy did not begin with rights. It began with infrastructure, education, military readiness, and the slow expansion of civil institutions. Freedom was not granted all at once. It was earned, painstakingly, through law, discipline, and patience. Order came first. And only then did liberty last.

Even liberalism's founding thinkers knew this. Hobbes feared chaos more than tyranny. Locke, the father of modern liberal theory, did not begin with liberty. He began with law. Freedom, he believed, existed inside a structure of rights, not outside it. No serious liberal tradition has ever treated freedom as self-sustaining. Only modern ones do.

This is why order is not simply one value among others. It is the foundation upon which every other liberal defence depends. The liberal creed cannot be defended unless it first exists. And it cannot exist unless something coherent, enforceable, and strong has been built to hold it up. This is the first act of defence. Every tooth of liberalism grows from this root.

Freedom must rest on something, and that something is structure. Strong borders, not out of fear but out of fairness. Strong laws, not to crush dissent but to contain exploitation. Strong institutions, not to impose ideology but to prevent its capture. Strong education, not just in rights, but in the duties that give those rights meaning.

This is not authoritarianism. It is civic architecture. A republic is not built on feelings, but on frameworks. And those frameworks require enforcement: clear, consistent, and purposeful. Order is not the enemy of liberty. It is its guardian. The wolves do not fear words. They fear boundaries enforced with courage.

The fantasy that freedom flourishes without rules is not only naïve, it is dangerous. When rules dissolve, the strong dominate. Extremists shout the loudest. Corporations exploit ambiguity. Institutions lose confidence. And moderates, the stewards of the liberal order, become disengaged or irrelevant. A democracy without discipline becomes a stage for its own undoing.

Today's liberal institutions have grown timid. Afraid to judge, to be firm, to draw the line between tolerating dissent and enabling collapse. In that vacuum of conviction, the loudest voices win. Institutions now confuse permissiveness with fairness, silence with neutrality, softness with virtue. But restraint is not cowardice. It is cowardice that invites collapse.

The wolves are already here. They do not wear boots or badges. They run platforms. They brand sabotage as activism. When corporate systems reward outrage, when extremists call for collapse without repair, when public discourse becomes performance and courts become theatre, it is not liberty that flourishes. It is spectacle. And spectacle cannot hold a republic.

We are already seeing this erosion. When courts are ignored, when protests turn to riots, when public discourse becomes unreality, and when laws are gamed rather than followed, it is not a sign of democratic vitality. It is democratic fragility. Whether in Britain, America, or elsewhere, a society that loses its taste for enforcement will soon lose its taste for liberty, too.

In Britain, the signs are plain. Shoplifting is now so routine that some retailers have stopped even reporting it. Police warn against investigating burglaries unless violence is involved. Councils teeter on bankruptcy, unable to enforce the basics of order. Citizens see rules bent without consequence, and the message is clear: restraint is optional. That perception does more damage than statistics, for once the sense of order is lost, faith in liberty soon follows.

This is why Sheepdog Liberalism accepts the burden of enforcement. We do not apologise for upholding rules. We do not retreat from the word "structure." We understand that liberty is a product, not a precursor. It comes after order, not before it.

The sheepdog is not noble because it barks. It is noble because it bears the burden no one else will. Enforcement lacks glamour, and order offers no prestige or romance. But without them, freedom collapses. Someone must stand where others will not.

The sheepdog does not glorify control. It does not seek applause. It understands that without enforcement, freedom becomes performance. And performance cannot hold a society together. Liberalism is not maintained by goodwill or gestures. It endures only through the defence against chaos, through rules that mean something and the courage to enforce them.

We choose structure not because it is easy, but because it is necessary. We will teach it, and we will defend it. Because without it, freedom is not threatened. It is gone.

Order: the first defence. The tooth that keeps chaos at bay. Without it, liberty crumbles.

When the sheepdog returned, fences lay in ruin, the flock drifting through open gaps. Freedom had become fragility. Patiently, he began restoring the lines; not walls to confine but boundaries of trust to hold the field together. At first the posts bent and wavered, too thin to carry the weight. Yet as the frame rose and the first lines held, the pasture gained what it had lost: a foundation on which true renewal could begin.

Order, they realised, is not the enemy of freedom. It is its foundation.

Tooth 2: Borders Guard Liberty

Freedom does not exist in the abstract. It exists in a place, and that place must be defined.

Without borders, there is no nation. Without a nation, there is no citizenship, and without citizenship, there are no rights to defend – only preferences to negotiate.

The liberal state is not an open field; it is a walled garden. And those walls are not a rejection of freedom, but its condition. They define the space in which law applies, where responsibility is shared, and where rules are the same for all.

A house without walls is not a home. When every door is unlatched, every window left open, and every rule made negotiable, the result is not generosity. It is uncertainty. No one knows who lives there, no one knows who is inside, and no one knows whose rules apply. What begins as openness quickly becomes confusion. What should feel like sanctuary begins to feel like risk. This is what liberalism becomes when it abandons immigration control. Not a refuge. Not a home. A contested space where those who cherish shared values must live beside those who reject or undermine them. A society that cannot define who it is and who it is not, will eventually become whatever its strongest intruder wants it to be.

This is the logic of borderlessness. It romanticises openness while eroding obligation. It offers welcome without weight and belonging without buy-in. But no liberal order can survive if it does not know who it serves or who is willing to serve it.

We have already seen this strain in action. In the European migration crisis of 2015, overwhelmed borders and undefined asylum processes caused fractures across the continent. Far right movements surged. Centrist governments collapsed. The moral high ground became politically untenable. It was not the presence of migrants alone that sparked reaction. It was the sense that the system had no limits, no cohesion, and no plan.

History makes this even clearer. Rome did not fall by conquest alone. It fell as its borders blurred, as citizenship was extended too cheaply, as loyalty fractured. Tribes became mercenaries, and the mercenaries became citizens without responsibility. The empire's interior rotted before its enemies breached the gate.

By contrast, the post-war liberal democracies that thrived, such as Austria and Norway, did so by setting clear immigration terms, tying entry to integration, and maintaining strong civic norms. Austria's citizenship process demands language, contribution, and commitment to national values. Norway combines openness with civic education and service requirements, ensuring that entry comes with responsibility as well as welcome. These systems prove that boundaries are not a rejection of generosity, but the condition that makes generosity sustainable.

Even John Stuart Mill warned that representative government required a united public. A people with shared commitments, not just coexisting communities. Borders are not simply lines on a map. They are a moral contract between the state and its citizens. A liberal society must be able to say: you may join us, but only if you join the project. This is why borders are a tooth. They are the line the wolves cannot cross, the proof that liberty is not up for negotiation.

We must remember this: to invite someone into your home is a virtue, but to invite them into a house you cannot maintain is not hospitality. It is collapse disguised as kindness. You cannot share what you do not protect. You cannot build common ground if no one agrees where the ground begins.

Today, we have forgotten that distinction. We treat all boundaries as burdens. We fear that drawing a line means losing our compassion. But compassion without condition becomes chaos, and a borderless liberalism quickly becomes a platform exploited by actors who neither love it nor intend to defend it.

The wolves understand this. They use open systems to advance illiberal goals. Authoritarians fund think tanks and media operations inside free societies. Religious fundamentalists invoke their rights to erode the rights of others. Corporations shop for the weakest jurisdictions and import labour without loyalty. Global platforms override national rules. And the liberal state, afraid to seem exclusive, invites its very own undoing.

This is not xenophobia. It is civic realism. The sheepdog does not guard the gate because it hates the outsider. It guards the gate because it knows that a shared space requires shared rules, and that rules require boundaries.

To defend borders is to defend fairness. If you do not control who joins the game, you cannot make the game fair. You cannot protect equality before the law if you no longer know who the law binds.

The sheepdog does not build walls from fear. It builds doors with locks. Locks that open when someone knocks and says, "I want to live by your values, under your laws, with your people." And then proves it.

We must not confuse borders with cruelty, nor openness with virtue.

A liberal society is not liberal because it lacks boundaries. It is liberal because it defines them justly, applies them fairly, and defends them without shame.

We will welcome the stranger, but not the saboteur.

We will integrate the new, but not dissolve the old.

We will open the gate, but not abandon the fence.

Because a society that does not guard what it loves, will lose it.

Borders: the boundary that holds. For without them, you cannot tell those who share liberty's burden from those who would devour it.

The sheepdog walked the perimeter in silence, tracing the boundaries he had rebuilt. At each gate he weighed what entered and what left. Where once the flock had wandered without question, now they paused, considered, and asked: who comes for shelter, and who comes to spoil? In time they understood that generosity without judgment was not kindness, but surrender.

And so, they kept the door open, but never unguarded.

Tooth 3: Values, the Tribe That Defends

Liberalism cannot survive on procedure alone. A functioning democracy needs more than laws, votes, and rights. It needs a shared moral core. A tribe of values.

This tribe is not based on blood, language, or ancestry. It is based on belief: that individuals have dignity, that speech must be free, that law must be impartial, and that pluralism is not chaos, but a virtue. These are not customs, they are convictions. And if a society does not defend them, it will be overrun by those who don't share them and don't intend to.

Values are the tooth that stops the wolves from claiming neutrality as a shield. Without shared values, the gate is unguarded, and every predator enters under the banner of "difference."

Imagine a school where students are taught that no culture is better than any other. That every value is simply perspective. That honour killings and free speech are equally valid. That stoning a dissenter and tolerating disagreement are simply different "ways of life." What would that school produce? Not thinkers. Not citizens. Fragments. People who speak past each other, live beside each other, and owe nothing to one another.

Now imagine a neighbourhood where liberal norms are ignored in the name of sensitivity. Where forced marriage, female genital mutilation, or antisemitism are tolerated as "community practices." Where law bends to avoid being accused of discrimination. Where those who try to uphold shared standards are accused of bigotry. This does not produce harmony. It produces parallel lives and moral confusion. And in the cracks between cultures, predators grow bold.

This is what a society becomes when it mistakes multiculturalism for moral relativism. It becomes a collection of parallel moral worlds, and liberalism, meant to be the shared space between those worlds, dissolves into noise.

The tribe of values is the fence that keeps liberty coherent. Without it, there is no "we" to defend, only fragments waiting to be conquered.

We have seen this danger before. In Lebanon, once a model of diversity, shared identity collapsed into sectarianism. Schools, neighbourhoods, and parties all fractured along religious lines. There was no "we" left, only "us" and "them." And soon, war. Not because there were too many groups, but because there were too few shared values.

We have seen it in Britain, too. In Rotherham and other towns, girls were raped and trafficked while authorities looked the other way, afraid that enforcing the law might upset cultural sensitivities. This is what happens when fear of judgment becomes stronger than moral clarity.

By contrast, civic nations like Switzerland and Singapore built unity through shared ideals. You could become "Swiss" or "Singaporean" not by ancestry, but by joining the creed. Learn the language, serve the community, uphold the rules. It was imperfect. It still is. But it gave these nations cohesion that diversity alone cannot.

Rousseau warned that a republic must educate the citizen not just in skills, but in spirit. That liberty is not simply the absence of control, but the presence of shared virtue. If liberalism is neutral on all values, it cannot teach its own, and if it cannot teach, it cannot last.

John Rawls, the great liberal philosopher of the 20th century, wrote that a just society is one that can be agreed upon by all reasonable citizens. But if society is too fractured to agree on what justice means, then even liberalism's foundations begin to split. Public reason becomes private rhetoric, and reason itself loses trust.

Today, this is precisely the crisis we face. Institutions are afraid to define what is good. Schools fear "imposing" values. Cultural critics equate moral judgment with bigotry. And so, liberal societies raise citizens who inherit rights but not responsibilities, freedoms but not purpose.

The wolves exploit this vacuum. Religious extremists preach against liberty inside the liberties we grant them. Ideologues call tolerance "oppression" and bend pluralism into submission. Corporations promote amoral relativism, reducing all values to consumption. And cultural institutions, afraid to offend, retreat from any standard at all.

A society that believes in nothing cannot resist those who believe in something; even if that something is violence, domination, or theocracy.

A people who refuse to say what they stand for cannot defend it when it is attacked. Silence is not neutrality, it is surrender. And in that silence, the wolves advance.

This is why Sheepdog Liberalism insists: we must teach what we are. We must name our values, explain them, defend them, and expect them to be upheld. Not as one tradition among many, but as the foundation of liberal order.

This means asserting that not all practices are equal. That liberal norms are not neutral. They are moral. That those who reject the equality of women, the dignity of LGBT citizens, the rule of law, or the freedom of speech are not expressing a different perspective. They are rejecting the tribe.

The sheepdog does not enforce ideology. It enforces boundaries of value. You may believe what you like. But if you act in ways that violate liberal principles, you are not simply different. You are dangerous.

To defend values is not to abandon tolerance. It is to give tolerance meaning. It is to say: you are welcome here, but not to tear this down. You may criticise but not persecute. You may dissent but not destroy.

We must not confuse moral clarity with moral arrogance; the

tribe of values is open to all those who respect what it is built on.

This tooth denies the Islamist and fascist wolves a moral vacuum. Liberalism without values becomes liberalism without meaning, a skeleton without a soul. And souls do not survive in isolation. They survive in community. In teaching. In expectation. In defence.

We will not apologise for our values, we will not water them down to avoid discomfort, and we will not trade them for tolerance that demands our silence. We believe in free speech, in individual dignity, in the equality of women and men, in the right to dissent, in the rule of law, and in the duty to defend them.

This is why values are a tooth: they close the gate that wolves slip through when a society refuses to say what it stands for. With values named and defended, the wolves find no vacuum to fill.

We are not a blood tribe. We are a values tribe. And this tribe defends liberty.

Yet fences alone were insufficient. Boundaries could hold danger back, but only conviction could hold the field together. The sheepdog turned his gaze inward, toward what the pasture itself had forgotten: dignity, respect, pluralism, and impartial justice. At first the field seemed uncertain, fearing that shared values might divide rather than unite. But clarity returned. Strength lay not in coexistence alone, but in conviction.

At twilight the flock gathered, not out of fear but with intention. They renewed the customs they had neglected, marked the lines of trust, and spoke without apology of what they stood for. From the hill the sheepdog watched as the pasture steadied into harmony once more. It was no longer merely a flock but a fellowship, shaped not by blood but by belief.

A tribe that knew what it defended and why it would endure.

Tooth 4: Citizenship, the Duty That Sustains

Liberalism was not built by customers. It was built by citizens.

A citizen is not someone who merely enjoys rights; a citizen participates, contributes, defends, and decides. A consumer asks, "What do I get?" A citizen asks, "What can I give?"

This is why citizenship is a tooth. Wolves thrive where people behave as customers, but they falter where citizens act as stewards. Consumerism leaves the field scattered. Citizenship closes ranks.

When we replace citizenship with consumerism, we reduce politics to preference, identity to lifestyle, and freedom to shopping. We begin to treat countries like brands, laws like terms of service, neighbours like service providers. And when something breaks, we don't fix it. We complain, or we switch platforms.

Imagine a town in which people complain about crime but never vote, where schools are underfunded but no one volunteers. Neighbours don't know each other, yet they argue online. Local decisions are judged not by what strengthens the community, but what increases property value. In this town, freedom still exists in theory. But in practice, it has been replaced by expectation without contribution.

This is not democracy; it is political consumerism that leaves us atomised and impatient. Fragile in the face of real responsibility.

We saw this begin to unfold in the 1980s and 90s, as neoliberal ideology turned democratic participation into customer satisfaction. "The market will solve it" became the answer to every question. Public space shrank. Obligation declined. The citizen was rebranded as a taxpayer. And freedom became the right to buy and complain.

In that vacuum, the wolves find entry. They exploit apathy, divide atomised individuals, and turn a public of customers into prey.

But consumer freedom is not political freedom. The former satisfies; the latter sustains.

When Hurricane Katrina hit New Orleans in 2005, thousands were stranded. Institutions failed and infrastructure collapsed whilst many watched, not knowing how to help because they had never been asked to. The logic of consumerism had trained them to expect delivery, not duty. The idea that the citizen has a role beyond the ballot box or market had been lost.

Contrast that with Finland. Every citizen there undergoes

national service and civic training. It is not about militarism, it's about expectation. The Finn is not just a taxpayer or shopper. They are a stakeholder. And in times of crisis, whether war or pandemic, that matters. Because you cannot mobilise a population that has only been taught to demand, not defend.

There are modern examples of resistance to this drift toward apathy and civic decay. In Taiwan, students are taught digital literacy and civic responsibility from a young age. In Estonia, digital citizenship includes not just rights but obligations. In Switzerland, service and democratic participation go hand in hand. These societies still teach that freedom carries weight. That the state is not a service provider, but a shared commitment.

This is why thinkers like Hannah Arendt warned that freedom requires a public realm, where citizens act and take responsibility together. The private realm is for need. The public realm is for meaning. Michael Sandel added more recently that a market society is not the same as a market economy. When market logic takes over every part of life – politics, education, identity – it hollows out the common good.

Today, this erosion is everywhere. Voter turnout drops. Volunteerism fades. Institutions beg for engagement. The citizen retreats into entertainment, outrage, and purchase. We click. We complain. We consume. But we no longer build.

In Britain, turnout at local elections has collapsed to below a third in many towns. Councils struggle to fill civic roles. Once-proud traditions of local volunteering and community associations wither, replaced by online outrage with no consequence. Citizens still complain about decline, but fewer are willing to carry the duties that make decline reversible. The state is treated as a service provider, not a shared project. And when duty disappears, the wolves do not need to attack. They only need to wait.

And when this happens, the wolves enter.

Corporations prefer consumers to citizens. Consumers do not organise or regulate. They don't resist. They browse. And they obey.

Authoritarians benefit, too. Consumer societies are fragmented and isolated and easily distracted. When the public forgets how to act together, it is easier to divide them. Easier to suppress. Easier to replace substance with spectacle.

Ideology thrives in this vacuum. People who no longer participate in real citizenship become vulnerable to movements that promise identity without responsibility, belonging without service and morality without effort.

The sheepdog knows freedom is not a delivery. It is a discipline.

It must be practiced. It must be shared. It must be earned.

This means building institutions where citizens don't just vote but serve. It means rethinking education, not just to train, but to prepare stewards of democracy. It means reasserting that to live in a democracy is to carry its weight, not to outsource it.

Citizenship must be cultivated. Through service, through education, through duty. Without that, people drift into consumption, and the wolves enter through apathy.

It means rejecting the idea that the state is a vending machine. It is a shared project. And those who inherit it must contribute to it. Through service. Through knowledge. Through sacrifice.

We must not fear words like duty or obligation. They are not authoritarian; they are what keep liberty from decaying into drift.

Liberalism is not a subscription. It is a covenant.

We will teach our young not just to express, but to serve.

We will ask not only what rights they enjoy, but what responsibilities they accept.

We will reawaken the identity of the citizen, not as a consumer of policy, but as a builder of society.

This tooth denies the wolves their easiest prey. A public of citizens cannot be bought, distracted, or divided in the same way a market of consumers can.

Because no republic can survive when its people forget they are its stewards.

We are not clients of the state.
We are not customers of democracy.
We are not entitled shareholders demanding better perks.
We are citizens. And the burden of citizenship is not a cost. It is the price of freedom.

Citizenship: the duty that sustains. For without it, liberty collapses into drift, and the wolves claim the field.

Yet some within the pasture had grown content, treating its soil as sustenance rather than stewardship. The sheepdog turned to them with steady resolve and reminded them that grazing was not enough. The field required care. At first there was hesitation, but soon the flock began tending the grass, repairing what had weakened, restoring what had been left unattended.

In time the need for reminders faded. The flock strengthened the fences before they failed, shared what they had before it spoiled, and looked to one another with a sense of duty rather than doubt. The pasture, once only a place of feeding, became a field they protected, for they understood now that it was theirs.

Not to own, but to serve.

Tooth 5: Economic Sovereignty, the Integrity That Shields

A nation that cannot control its economy cannot control its destiny.

Markets matter, but so does morality. And when economic policy forgets the moral foundation of a republic, liberalism begins to rot from the inside out.

Economic liberalism was never meant to be surrender. Trade was meant to create interdependence, not dependence. Capital was meant to serve communities, not extract from them. This is why sovereignty is a tooth. Wolves thrive where livelihoods collapse, but they falter where nations keep their prosperity anchored to their people.

But for decades, liberal democracies have allowed financial logic to override moral logic, treating national sovereignty as inefficient, cultural resilience as optional, and citizenship as a cost centre.

This is not freedom. It is drift.

Imagine a small town in which the factory closes, the shops empty, the young leave, and the only thing growing is despair. The market has moved on, but the people remain. Their skills are no longer useful. Their pride is no longer respected. Their vote, their voice, their value; all feel irrelevant. The politicians tell them to retrain. The companies tell them to move. The culture tells them to stop complaining. And eventually, the wolves arrive with a simpler offer: blame someone, burn something, belong.

Now zoom out. Imagine a country that builds none of its own infrastructure. It imports energy, exports value and relies on foreign supply chains for its daily life. When crisis hits – war, pandemic, natural disaster – there is nothing left to stand on. No reserve. No resilience. Only exposure. This is not liberalism. It is liquidation.

This is what economic liberalism without civic loyalty produces: collapse disguised as progress.

We've seen this cycle across the liberal world. In Britain and America, industrial decline became moral decline because the market was treated as a god, not a tool. In Europe, austerity measures punished the vulnerable while rewarding speculative capital. In developing democracies, foreign direct investment often comes without dignity; extracting resources, skimming profits, and undermining labour protections. Liberal states signed away leverage for efficiency. And in doing so, they weakened the social fabric. In that weakness, the wolves found their opening. They prey on hollow economies because hollow economies cannot defend citizens from despair.

We see it in modern crises, too. During COVID-19, even wealthy democracies discovered they couldn't produce their own medical supplies. During energy shocks, nations that outsourced capacity found themselves at the mercy of autocrats. And in global food systems, we see the dangerous fragility of "just-in-time" logic when supply chains crack and the shelves go bare.

This was not inevitable. It was ideological. The story told was that open markets would lead to open societies. But when global trade erodes local cohesion, when finance outpaces responsibility, when citizens feel like strangers in their own economy, liberalism becomes the thing to punish, not protect.

The wolves are not abstract. They wear names. When Chinese autocrats control your energy supply, your liberty is hostage. When Amazon and other monopolies replace your high street, community collapses into consumption. When speculative capital treats homes as assets rather than dwellings, citizens become tenants of forces they cannot vote out. And when firms like Palantir hold your health records, police data, and military contracts, sovereignty slides quietly into technocratic fascism. Decisions that once belonged to parliaments and courts drift into the hands of corporations whose power is neither elected nor restrained. Wolves exploit dependence; and dependence, once built, is almost impossible to reverse.

The original liberal theorists never believed in markets without morals. Adam Smith warned that commerce needed ethical anchors. John Stuart Mill believed the state must temper inequality to preserve liberty. Even Hayek, a fierce defender of markets, saw the state's role in preserving the rule of law as essential. What we practice now is not classical liberalism. It is corporate technocracy dressed in liberal language.

And the wolves thrive in this vacuum.

Populists channel rage, but offer no plan. Authoritarians promise dignity, but only deliver control. Corporations centralise power, but offload risk. And while liberals hesitate to draw moral lines around the economy, others draw them with fire.

Sheepdog Liberalism does not accept this drift. We reject the idea that the market is morally neutral. We reject the myth that globalisation is inevitable. We believe sovereignty is not just about borders, it is about economic self-respect.

This means reasserting that economics is not separate from ethics, that prosperity without dignity is not peace, that trade without reciprocity is not partnership, and that citizenship without economic recognition is not freedom.

It means asking different questions. Not simply what is efficient, but what is just. Not only what maximises output, but what reinforces unity. Not just what grows the economy, but what grows the republic.

A healthy economy is not just productive. It is participatory, it rewards work, it protects the vulnerable, it builds resilience, and most importantly, it resists domination, whether from multinational monopolies or hostile foreign capital.

Sovereignty without economic integrity is paper-thin. A republic cannot function if its people are economically abandoned and told to be grateful, and liberalism cannot endure if its material benefits are decoupled from civic identity.

The sheepdog does not bark only at the borders; it guards the shared prosperity, too. It knows that liberty requires independence, not just of laws, but of livelihood.

We will not surrender our civic strength to financial expediency. We will not apologise for protecting the systems that make our society whole.

We believe in trade, in growth, and in markets, but only when they serve nations, not replace them. This tooth denies the wolves the power to buy what they cannot conquer. A republic that keeps its economy sovereign keeps its liberty intact.

Economic sovereignty as integrity. Or liberalism will be bought out from beneath us.

The sheepdog found the pasture depleted and its strength compromised. The flock had yielded control to wolves disguised in wool, trading stability for hollow assurances. With patience, he restored what had been lost and reminded the field of its own capacity. The soil was replanted, the boundaries renewed, and the field began once more to sustain itself. Gradually, the pasture recovered its pride, knowing its prosperity depended on its own discipline.

It no longer traded its grain for trinkets or borrowed feed. It measured its worth not in size but in soundness. The wolves circled but found no weakness to exploit.

The pasture had learned that prosperity is not measured by abundance but by integrity, and that integrity is what shields liberty.

Tooth 6: Justice, the Balance That Holds

Liberalism cannot stand on ideals alone. It stands because people believe the rules are fair. Fairness is not an ornament of the system; it is its balance. It is what convinces the citizen that the law protects them as much as it restrains them, that their neighbour is bound by the same obligations, that those in power are judged by the same scales. When that belief dies, wolves do not need to break the fence; the sheep open it themselves.

This is why justice is a tooth. It closes the wolves' favourite opening: grievance. Wolves feed on cynicism. They whisper that the game is rigged, that the law is for some but not for others, that the strong bend rules while the weak are crushed by them. But when fairness is visible, grievance cannot divide. Where the scales are level, the wolves starve.

History shows the danger when fairness falters. Rome collapsed not from invasion alone but from corruption, as law became a currency of patronage. Weimar Germany still had courts, but extremists were indulged while moderates bore the weight; public trust cracked, and fascism marched in. By contrast, post-war Germany rebuilt legitimacy by insisting on accountability, however painful. South Africa bound its grief to process in truth and reconciliation, preventing violence from finishing the work.

Britain knows this truth as well. Fairness is our civic instinct; the queue, the apology, the expectation that rules apply the same whether high or low. When policing looks uneven, when inquiries drag, when scandals like Grenfell or the Post Office show that power shields itself, that instinct curdles into cynicism. And cynicism is where the wolves recruit. Because people do not want peace; they want justice. Peace without justice is only silence, and silence is what the wolves fill.

Today in Britain, nothing illustrates this more viscerally than the small boats crisis. The numbers are a fraction of overall immigration, yet the anger it sparks is disproportionate. Why? Because it feels like injustice. Citizens see veterans waiting for housing while asylum seekers are placed in hotels. They see disabled people battling bureaucracy for basic support while those who entered outside the rules appear to receive more. It is not the scale but the principle: that those who play by the rules are punished, while those who don't are rewarded. That sense of injustice corrodes trust faster than statistics can correct it, and it is precisely what parties like Reform exploit. A single issue, however small in proportion, can sway a national election when it strikes at the heart of fairness.

But Britain has also shown how justice, fairly applied, can renew belief. The suffragettes won not only votes for women, but trust that the system could evolve to match its ideals. Beveridge's reforms after the war turned fairness into welfare, binding liberty to security. Even in our own time, the Supreme Court's ruling against prorogation in 2019 showed the public that no government, however powerful, stood above the law. These moments mattered not only for their outcomes, but because they reminded the flock that the scales still worked.

The old liberals knew this. Locke tied liberty to impartial law so that the magistrate's will could never replace right. Montesquieu warned that liberty demanded the separation of powers to prevent corruption. Rawls, in our own age, framed justice as fairness, knowing that stability depends on rules people can accept even when outcomes cut against them. All agreed: without trust in fairness, freedom itself collapses.

Today, that trust thins. Policing is accused of double standards. Politicians sneer of "two-tier justice." Regulators pursue the small and spare the large. Inquiries drift until truth feels delayed into irrelevance. And in that vacuum of fairness, populists offer vengeance, theocrats demand purity, corporations game the rules. Wolves do not need to lie when justice looks crooked; they only need to point.

This is why justice is not an ornament, but a tooth. Once citizens lose belief in fairness, they withdraw consent. Law no longer commands respect; it must be imposed by force. And a democracy that relies only on enforcement has already begun to die.

The sheepdog cannot allow this. Its tooth is fairness itself: not the promise of perfection, but the visible insistence that rules apply to all. That sight, more than rhetoric, convinces the flock to stand together and denies the wolves their prey.

Justice, the balance that holds. Without it, liberty tilts, grievance festers, and the wolves inherit the field.

In the dim light of evening the pasture stirred with unease. Some believed the fence bent for a few while others were turned away. The sheepdog walked the boundary, testing each post, measuring every claim alike. He listened before he judged and weighed before he acted. His work was quiet but exacting, seen by all, favoured by none. When dawn came the field stood level again. Those who had doubted trusted the fence once more, and those who had been overlooked knew they were counted.

Beyond the tree line the wolves watched and did not move, for there was nothing crooked left to trade.

Tooth 7: Institutions, the Immune System That Protects

Liberal societies do not stand because their ideas are beautiful. They stand because their institutions hold.

Ideas can ignite change, but it is institutions that give that change permanence. Courts turn rights from aspiration into protection. Elections transform consent into legitimate authority. Regulators keep markets from sliding into predation. Together, they form the immune system of liberalism, steady in pace, modest in profile, yet indispensable to its survival.

This is why institutions are a tooth. Wolves thrive where systems fail, but they falter where rules hold, however slowly or imperfectly. Institutions deny them the easy prey of chaos.

When they work, we hardly notice them. When they fail, everything else begins to fail with them. A society without functioning institutions is not free; it is exposed. Step into a courthouse where the roof leaks, the docket runs years behind, and no one can tell you why your claim disappeared. Visit a town where police are feared but not trusted, where the election office stands empty, where inspectors appear only if bribed. This is institutional decay: not a dramatic collapse, but the daily corrosion of belief. And once belief is gone, order soon follows.

In a country where courts are politicised, parliaments paralysed, public services gutted, and regulators captured, citizens stop expecting fairness and start expecting chaos. Trust collapses, and into that vacuum flows power; claimed by whoever can shout the loudest, spend the most, or threaten the best. The rules still exist, but no one believes they will be applied evenly. Procedure still happens, but it produces only delay and dysfunction. In that climate, people turn to strongmen, slogans, or conspiracies, to anything that feels simpler than an institution that no longer works.

The immune system of a republic does not fail all at once. It fails organ by organ. Venezuela's rulers packed the courts and rigged elections, and in doing so, hollowed out the very institutions meant to protect the public. In Hungary and Poland, populists hollowed out judicial independence under the banner of reform. In the United States and the UK, partisan warfare has turned legislatures into battlegrounds where institutions are not shielded from emotion but overwhelmed by it. Once institutions become partisan property, they no longer mediate conflict; they weaponise it.

The original defenders of liberalism understood this. Montesquieu warned that liberty required separation of powers not as a formality, but as a safeguard against corruption. Madison argued that ambition must counter ambition so that no person could be trusted with unbalanced power. Popper wrote that the mark of an open society was not its perfection, but its ability to correct mistakes without collapse. All understood that structure does more than just organise freedom, it protects it from erosion.

Today, institutions are mocked as slow, boring, and bureaucratic. But slowness can be insulation, rather than failure. Bureaucracy can be protection, not control. Institutions exist not to thrill us, but to outlast us. That is why the wolves attack them.

Populists treat institutions as obstacles, delegitimising courts, parliaments, election bodies, and public health agencies. They brand them deep states, conspiracies, cabals, then replace them with personality cults, instant referenda, or unchecked executive rule. Corporations capture them from within, rewriting regulation, stacking advisory panels, flooding campaigns with money, and turning compliance into farce. They do not have to destroy institutions; only drain their independence.

And once drained, the wolves walk in freely – not through revolution, but through resignation. A hollowed immune system cannot resist infection.

Citizens watch, lose trust, and withdraw. They assume every institution is corrupt or compromised, so when the moment comes to defend them, they do not.

The danger is that decay never looks like collapse until it does. Institutions rot slowly, quietly, in ways the public barely notices. Case backlogs lengthen, regulators stall, small rules stop being enforced. Trust ebbs bit by bit, until the body of the republic can no longer fight off even the smallest fever. By the time the wolves arrive, the system is too weakened to resist. And collapse that once felt unthinkable suddenly looks inevitable.

The sheepdog does not worship institutions, but it understands their role. It defends them when they are mocked, when they falter, when they fall short. It knows that guarding a flawed court is better than no court at all, and that preserving a slow bureaucracy is better than letting rage make the rules. It holds the line, so others do not have to. It understands that no free society can survive without mechanisms that outlast moods, and that even flawed institutions are better than rule by flair. Liberalism is not maintained by sentiment; it is maintained by structure.

That means teaching what institutions are, not just what they do. It means fighting for reform without surrendering integrity, punishing corruption without abandoning the body when the immune system falters, and reawakening public loyalty not to parties or people, but to the system itself. Institutions are not relics; they are scaffolding. Without them, no republic stands.

They are not cages; they are commons, places where strangers agree to settle differences without war, share power without fear, and coexist without collapse. They are what stands between liberalism and tribalism. This tooth hardens the immune system the wolves fear most: our institutions.

We reject the fashion that treats rules as oppression. We will not confuse compromise with cowardice. We will not embrace shortcuts that promise renewal but deliver collapse. We believe in reform grounded in structure, in critique offered in good faith, and in defending the system not because it is perfect, but because it is worth protecting.

The sheepdog does not guard perfection. It guards the conditions for renewal.

Institutions: the immune system that protects. Without them, liberalism does not heal from its wounds; it perishes from every passing fever, and the wolves finish what decay began.

The sheepdog worked tirelessly, reinforcing the barns, the shaded places, the quiet corners where disputes had once been settled with care. Yet the damage ran deeper than one guardian could mend. He lifted his head and howled, not in fear but in summons. From beyond the hills, other sheepdogs answered. Together they watched over the pasture, guarding not only the flock but the spaces where it gathered and healed. The flock watched as calm returned, not imposed but protected, not through force but through vigilance and shared duty. They saw now that their safety rested not only in fences but in the quiet ground where trust could grow.

And they understood that no single guardian, however loyal, could defend the field alone.

Tooth 8: Formation, the Shield of the Liberal Soul

Liberalism is not passed down by blood. It is passed down by teaching and by example. A free society does not survive by accident. It survives because each generation is formed in discipline, knowledge, and responsibility, to defend what it has inherited.

Every society is one generation away from forgetting what made it free. And in a liberal society, where power is not enforced by fear but sustained by belief, formation becomes more than instruction. It becomes defence. Wolves exploit drift, decadence, and amnesia. They advance where citizens are untaught. But they falter where the liberal soul is deliberately formed.

You cannot defend what you do not understand. And you will not defend what you have never been taught to value. Education without virtue produces clever cynics. Virtue without education produces earnest zealots. But when combined, they form the liberal soul: citizens who know their rights, respect their duties, and defend liberty with judgment, not just noise.

Imagine a classroom where students can name ten identities, but not the branches of government. Where every essay critiques power, but none explain how power is formed, shared, or limited. Where debate is performance, not persuasion. That is not education. It is collapse by confusion.

Now imagine a society where the rules still exist, but no one follows them unless forced. Where honesty is mocked as naïve, promises mean little, and truth splinters into private versions. That is not liberty. It is decadence.

History proves this point. Post-war Germany rebuilt itself not only through new institutions, but by teaching every child why tyranny had risen, and why it must never rise again. Post-war Japan embedded civic duty into its schools, tying prosperity to responsibility. By contrast, Weimar Germany educated its young in grievance but not in citizenship. It produced a literate society that still succumbed to barbarism because it lacked formation of the liberal soul. The lesson is clear: civilisation is not knowledge alone, but knowledge bound to duty.

Where civic formation is absent, other forces rush in. Social media rewards speed; liberal education once rewarded reflection. One builds reaction, the other resilience. Remove the latter, and the former dominates. In that vacuum grows radicalisation, tribalism, and manipulation. Wolves thrive on untrained souls.

A nation that does not form its citizens cannot sustain its freedom. It only keeps its population, waiting for the first strongman or zealot to teach them something firmer. Untaught means undefended, and undefended means conquered.

The old defenders of liberty understood this. Mill argued that education must cultivate independent judgment, not passive acceptance. Tocqueville saw that democracy survived only where citizens formed habits of service and association. Even Isaiah Berlin admitted that a society without inner guardrails collapses under its own licence. And today, Martha Nussbaum warns that education must form world citizens, able to imagine others' lives and live across difference. All of them understood that liberal institutions survive only when the liberal soul is renewed.

Formation closes the opening the wolves exploit. It trains citizens not just in knowledge but in judgment, not just in rights but in restraint. It teaches the will to say: "Just because I can, does not mean I should."

This is not about moral perfection. It is about moral expectation. The duty to know the system you inherit, so you can defend it when tested. Freedom is not self-justifying. It must be tempered, channelled, and earned every day, in how we live, in what we teach, and in the habits we honour.

Formation is not a luxury. It is the renewal of the liberal soul. What is not formed will not be remembered. What is not remembered will not be protected. And what is not protected will be lost.

Formation: the shield of the liberal soul. Without it, liberalism forgets itself, and the wolves inherit a people untrained to resist.

The sheepdog turned his gaze to the young pups trailing behind him, eager and untested. He walked with them through the pasture, showing where the fences weakened and how the wind could hide a wolf's approach. He taught them not only to bark, but to know when silence served better; not only how to act, but why their watch mattered and what would come if it failed.

Some within the pasture doubted such caution, believing danger was behind them. Yet seasons changed, and the wolves returned; new ones, quieter, cleverer. And this time the young dogs were ready.

The flock watched as the new generation held the line. They saw that defence was not instinct but discipline, and that wisdom, passed down with patience, was what kept the field secure.

Formation, they understood, was the shield of the liberal soul, the first warning before danger ever arrived.

Tooth 9: Restraint, the Leash That Protects

Liberalism must be defended. But it must be defended without becoming its own threat.

Tooth 9 exists to defend the moral boundary between liberalism and tyranny: the difference between force that protects liberty, and force that corrupts it. The sheepdog is necessary, but only so long as it remembers what it is guarding.

Because liberalism's immune system must be strong, but it must also be contained.

The sheepdog is not the wolf. But neither is it the lamb. It has teeth. And those teeth must remain under control. For wolves are not the only danger. A society without restraint breeds its own predators. The greatest threat is not the wolf outside the fence, but the wolf that citizens can become if discipline is lost.

In every liberal society there is a temptation: to protect liberty by force, to silence enemies in the name of peace, to enforce order without restraint.

But when the defender forgets the thing they are defending, liberalism does not die from weakness. It dies from overcorrection.

History is full of revolutions that became regimes. Guards who became tyrants. Emergencies that were never lifted. Constitutions rewritten in the name of security. Rights suspended for "just one crisis more." **The people, in their fear, became the very thing they resisted.**

This is what restraint guards against: not just collapse,

but capture – when the protectors stop protecting and start controlling.

That is why every serious liberal tradition has placed limits on its defenders. The U.S. Constitution separates powers not just to manage government, but to constrain its enforcers. The British model of civilian-led policing emerged not to fight crime harder but to fight it justly. And in post-authoritarian democracies from Chile to South Africa, new liberal orders embedded checks into their constitutions to ensure the defenders could never become dominators.

The constitution is not just a legal document. It is a philosophical restraint. A public oath that power may be used but never unaccountably.

That is why the sheepdog must remain leashed.

This means clear oversight. Defined limits. Civilian control of security. Review of emergency powers. Legal thresholds that cannot be gamed or ignored. A culture that teaches that power is always dangerous, even when it is yours.

It also means a citizenry that practices restraint in daily life: in speech, in protest, in politics. For the British are not passive sheep; they are sheepdogs, too. And if they abandon restraint, their passion can turn feral, their vigilance into vengeance. Restraint is the tooth that guards us not only from the wolves, but from becoming wolves ourselves.

To defend liberalism is not to abandon limits. It is to model them.

Because it is morally necessary. Authority without humility becomes abuse. Power without conscience becomes theatre. And law without restraint becomes tyranny. Liberalism is the only system that demands its own defenders be restrained, and that is what makes it worth defending.

The old liberals understood this.

John Locke argued that even in emergencies, the rule of law must return. Montesquieu believed that liberty depended not on the absence of force, but on its division. James Madison feared not only monarchy, but the unmoderated passions of defenders with too much reach. And Hannah Arendt warned that when the state demands loyalty above legality, liberalism is already lost.

All of them understood that the price of liberty is not just vigilance, it is restraint.

Imagine a society in which defenders of freedom adopt the tactics of authoritarians: spying without cause, censoring dissent, excusing violence against "the right targets." They claim to guard liberalism, but in their methods, they destroy its soul.

Liberalism is not sustained by panic. It is sustained by principle.

That means more than law. It means restraint. Proportion. The discipline to hold the line without crossing it.

The sheepdog must not become addicted to control. It must not confuse order with domination. It must not mistake criticism for sabotage.

In liberalism, the defender is bound by the very rules they protect. That is what makes us different from the wolves.

Restraint is not softness. It is the line that divides guardianship from domination. Without it, the sheepdog is indistinguishable from the wolf. And once that line is crossed, liberty is not defended but devoured in its name.

This does not mean weakness. It means calibration. The sheepdog must be strong, but never feral.

When protest turns violent, we defend the law, but not by outlawing protest. When extremists exploit free speech, we respond, but not by silencing everyone. When chaos tempts us to shut everything down, we pause, but do not freeze.

Liberalism requires enforcement. But it also requires reflection.

That reflection is what keeps force within bounds. It is what prevents the protectors from becoming the predators.

We will not defend liberty by destroying its institutions, nor preserve speech by punishing dissent, nor uphold law by abandoning its spirit.

We believe in force guided by judgment, shaped by restraint, and held in check by principle.

The sheepdog does not enjoy its power. It bears it.

If this duty is ignored, the results are never freedom. They are panic, paranoia, and repression. Societies spiral from vigilance into vengeance. The state becomes a hammer. And every disagreement looks like a nail.

Liberalism cannot survive the sheepdog unleashed.

Restraint is the leash that protects. It keeps the wolves at bay, and it keeps us from becoming wolves ourselves.

In his tireless patrol the sheepdog grew sharper, quicker to sense movement, louder in his warnings.

One evening, as the light faded, he caught a flicker at the edge of the flock. Ears raised, he charged. But just before his teeth struck, another sheepdog leapt between them. The flicker had been no wolf, but a shaken, startled lamb.

Breathless, he stepped back, eyes wide. He had almost done what the wolves could not. The older sheepdogs circled him, not with punishment, but with presence. They reminded him that the teeth of the guardian and the teeth of the wolf are cut from the same bone, and only discipline decides which they serve. Strength must never outrun judgment. Duty must never become rage.

And so, the sheepdog learned the hardest lesson of all: that guarding the flock meant guarding his own instincts, too.

From that day on, he watched with as much care inward as he did outward, so he would never become what he was trained to stop.

Tooth 10: Belonging, the House Worth Guarding

Sheepdog Liberalism is not just a defence. It is a construction project.

We are not here simply to hold the gates. We are here to build the home behind them. A republic strong in its laws, noble in its character, proud in its culture, and generous in its welcome. Every tooth that came before; every rule, every limit, every act of restraint, was not for the sake of restriction, but to make something lasting. Something liveable. Something loved.

Liberalism cannot survive as a policy spreadsheet. It must become a home.

Imagine a house in which every wall is built, but nothing is inside. The doors are secured, the systems run, but no one sings. No one gathers. No one believes. That is what hollow liberalism becomes: a structure without a soul. People stay out of habit, not love. Until one day, they don't. They drift to tribes, to faiths, to ideologies that promise to fill the void.

We have seen this emptiness before. In the late Soviet Union, the system still stood, but belief had died. Citizens followed the rules but mocked the purpose. And when the collapse came, no one rose to defend it. Because there was nothing left to defend.

But we have also seen what is possible. After the Second World War, West Germany rebuilt not just its economy, but its identity. It taught civic virtue, embraced shared responsibility, and created a liberalism of dignity and duty. Citizens did not just follow the law. They helped rebuild the house.

The early liberals knew this. Mill believed that liberty should elevate character. Benjamin Constant warned that modern freedom must retain the spirit of ancient civic life. Václav Havel, living under totalitarianism, called for a politics that could restore dignity through truth. All of them understood that liberalism is not just protection from power, it is participation in purpose.

Today, liberal societies are efficient but empty. Bureaucratic but joyless. They ask citizens for loyalty but give them no reason to care. Patriotism is mocked. National purpose is outsourced. Civic identity is fragmented. And into that void, movements emerge; nativist, populist, ideological, each promising belonging where liberalism offers only process.

The wolves promise meaning. They wear the mask of tradition, strength, or sacrifice. They whisper that liberalism is too thin to feed the soul. And wolves do not always enter through force; they enter through emptiness. When citizens feel unseen or unwanted, they listen. Not because they are disloyal, but because they are starved.

The sheepdog does not only defend. It builds.

It helps shape a nation that people want to guard. Through national service, civic holidays, sacred ceremonies, shared stories, and local institutions that mean something. It fights not just for order, but for orientation. It restores dignity to structure and warmth to belonging.

It does not apologise for patriotism. It renews it.

It builds a life worth guarding: a plaza filled with voices, a national day that binds strangers in ritual, a public square where argument and respect coexist. A place where liberalism is not just defended, but lived, and loved.

In Canada, new citizens swear their oath surrounded by their communities, a moment that binds law to belonging. In Finland, civic education teaches not just institutions, but how to live with others in difference. In Germany, public memory anchors the present in the lessons of the past. These are not abstract ideals. They are liberalism made visible through ritual, pride, and shared meaning.

We will not let liberalism become management without meaning. We will not defend systems that forget the soul. We will not guard a house we no longer remember how to live in.

In Britain, this loss is already felt. Civic parades fade. St George's Day passes barely marked. Local remembrance services thin as younger generations drift away. What once bound neighbours together in ritual is replaced by private distraction and online outrage. A nation without shared ceremony cannot renew its soul, and wolves step easily into the silence of meaning.

Sheepdog Liberalism believes in structure with spirit, liberty with dignity, and a house strong at the gate, warm at the hearth and filled with light.

This is what every tooth has guarded. This is what the sheepdog has always stood for; not just protection from collapse, but the creation of something worth standing in front of.

The only question left is: what will you help build?

Belonging is the house worth guarding. For even the best defences are worthless if they guard nothing at all.

At last, the fences held and the pasture knew stillness. Yet something felt unfinished. Safety alone was not enough. Together the sheepdogs helped raise places for gathering and celebration, spaces for ritual and rest. Warmth returned, and the pasture became not only secure but beloved. The flock understood that freedom endures only when it shelters something worth defending, a home they cherish.

Freedom, they learned, is not only something guarded, but something lived.

THE SHEEPDOG LIBERAL MANIFESTO

Between the Soul and the Shield

What you have read so far is the soul of Sheepdog Liberalism. The ideals, the philosophy, the moral ground on which it stands. But belief alone cannot defend a nation.

From this point on, we turn to what Sheepdog Liberalism looks like in the real world. To the work of building defences strong enough to guard the values we have spoken of, not in theory, but in policy, in structure, and in the everyday machinery of a free people.

I will not leave you with philosophy alone. The Shield and the Seal are written to show how these ideas live, how they act, how they protect, and how they can be renewed.

The following manifesto is written for the times I live in. The world will change, and with it, the shape of our answers must change too.

If these policies fail, they must be replaced.

If they age, they must be renewed.

For the Sheepdog spirit is not one of stubbornness, but of service, to guard the same truth through different storms. The principles remain, even if the fences must be rebuilt.

What matters is the end they serve:

A nation strong enough to defend liberty, and free enough to remain worth defending.

VOLUME III: The Shield

The Twelve Pillars of the Great Repair

The Great Repair: Paying Down Our Societal Debt

Liberal societies don't collapse in an instant. They erode. Quietly, slowly, and from within.

The threats we face today are real, but the greater danger is the one we created ourselves: the slow decay of the foundations that hold liberal society together. The wolves are not overwhelming the gates because they are strong. They are finding their way in because the walls have been left untended.

There's a concept in software engineering called **technical debt.** It refers to all the bugs, shortcuts, and compromises that build up when you prioritise speed over stability. At first, the system still runs. Nothing crashes. But over time, every function becomes slower, glitchier, more fragile. Eventually, the whole thing buckles, not from one flaw, but from too many layers of unresolved problems. In tech, you pay that debt by pausing the feature rush and dedicating a full cycle to repair, to stabilise the base; Britain needs the same.

Britain is now carrying **societal debt.**

For decades, we have postponed structural repair in favour of surface fixes. We've outsourced core industries, neglected civic institutions, substituted sentiment for seriousness, and replaced stewardship with spectacle. The mechanics of democracy, economy, and identity have frayed while we told ourselves the system was still fine.

And it worked… for a while.

The economy grew. Elections happened. Rights expanded. Public life looked intact. But beneath it all, the foundations were cracking.

Trust collapsed. Infrastructure aged into failure. Debt; economic, social, and moral, spiralled. The sense of shared purpose that once gave liberalism its strength began to dissolve. Public services thinned. Local identities weakened. Unguarded institutions drifted into capture or irrelevance.

That is the cost of societal debt. It is not just a budget deficit, it's a deficit of resilience, cohesion, and meaning. And the bill is now due.

This chapter is about **repair**.

Not slogans. Not abstract hopes. But the deliberate, grounded work of restoring what makes liberalism functional: reliable institutions, a sovereign economy, civic education, border integrity, a shared national identity, and the rule of law.

Repair means more than patching cracks. It means building back stronger so the walls are harder to breach, the gates open only by choice, and the home inside is worth defending.

This is the work of *The Shield*. And its strength comes from the twelve core Pillars, each one a part of the structure we must rebuild if Britain is to endure.

***

First Pillar – The Lock

Guardrails Before Governance

Before we govern, we guard.

A free society is not secure because it means well; it is secure because its guardrails hold when pressed. The Lock is the first defence: a constitutional barrier that binds power to principle before policy ever begins.

Policy built on shifting ground collapses. Policy anchored in law endures. Rights, once codified, cannot be bent by whim. Limits, once written, cannot be erased by mood. Without the Lock, every other defence is temporary.

The Five Turns of the Lock

1. **Civil Liberty & Equal Protection**
   Freedom must be fenced to be real.
   – Codify freedom of speech, conscience, assembly, and religion.
   – Entrench minority rights so they cannot be eroded by party fashion.

2. **Rule of Law & Judicial Independence**
   Law must sit above politics, or it becomes prey to it.
   – Guarantee impartial courts and prosecutors, immune from executive interference.
   – Enshrine judicial review as a constitutional safeguard.

3. **Democratic Limits**
   Elections are not theatre; they are transfers of power bound by rules.
   – Define electoral integrity, peaceful transfer, and transparent oversight.
   – Place hard limits on emergency powers and executive decrees.

4. **Civic Duties**
   Citizenship is not a subscription. It is a covenant.
   – Embed service, mentorship, and civic education as expectations, not extras.
   – Link rights with duties in constitutional form.

5. Anti-Capture & Sovereignty
If institutions are not defended, they are bought.
– Defend against corruption, foreign influence, and corporate capture.
– Require transparency and disclosure across parties, think tanks, and public bodies.

The wolves do not always arrive in tanks. They test the hinges. They slip through gaps. They exploit drift.

Without a written foundation, liberalism depends on convention, and convention bends under pressure.

This is why the Lock must come first. Without it, every other pillar rests on sand. With it, we secure the ground on which the rest of the Shield will stand.

Freedom does not guard itself. Where the law is unwritten, it is bent. Where rights are only conventions, they are eroded. A constitution is not parchment, but protection; the lock that ensures liberty cannot be picked by strongmen or auctioned to the highest bidder. Without it, every fence can be moved, every duty forgotten, every promise revoked. With it, the field holds, even when storms come.

But a shield made only of laws will crack under the weight of decay inside. Once the Lock is secure, the next defence is to Forge the strength behind it; an economy built not for drift, but for endurance.

Second Pillar: The Forge

The Civic Economy- Markets, Ownership & Mission

A forge does not burn to admire sparks. It tempers fire into steel. So too must an economy temper ambition into dignity, ownership, and endurance. Growth without meaning is drift. Wealth without ownership is dispossession. A nation that rents its homes, leases its tools, and imports its strength is not free. It is fragile.

For decades Britain has mistaken expansion for strength. GDP rose, but resilience fell. Wealth grew, but ownership shrank. The field looked fertile, but the roots thinned. This is not just economic failure. It is civic disinheritance. A society where citizens feel like passengers in their own economy cannot stand guard over it.

The Sheepdog Economy

Markets are not enemies, nor are they gods. They are tools. And tools must serve the nation. Enterprise builds when rules are fair. Innovation flourishes when citizens have a stake. But when appetite drifts unrestrained, markets become engines of extraction, devouring the pasture they need to live.

Sheepdog Liberalism believes in free enterprise, but not in freefall. In trade, but not servitude. In ownership, not absentee landlordism. A civic economy begins with sovereignty and ends with dignity; citizens who build, own, and share in what they depend upon.

The Five Fires of the Forge

1. **Reindustrialise with Purpose**
   A nation that outsources its tools outsources its future.
   – Strategic sectors must return to domestic control: energy, semiconductors, compute, biomaterials, advanced agriculture.
   – Public–private hubs should be built in regions hollowed by deindustrialisation, tying local revival to national resilience.
   – State investment must be "mission-led," not "growth for its own sake," anchored in place, purpose, and security.
   – Every new factory or lab should be measured not only in output, but in the roots it lays: apprentices trained, towns revitalised, pride restored.

2. **Sovereign Energy & Data**
   You cannot rent survival. You must own it. Energy is the lifeblood of a nation.
   – End foreign state ownership of nuclear plants, data centres, telecoms, and compute infrastructure.
   – Establish a National Energy Resilience Fund to build nuclear, hydrogen, and next-gen renewables at scale.

– Develop sovereign AI infrastructure: publicly owned data hubs, compute capacity, and ethical algorithms.
– Cheap, abundant power lowers the cost of R&D across biotech, quantum, and advanced manufacturing. A nation with surplus energy funds its future on its own terms.

3. Jobs with Dignity, Not Dependence
Work is not just income. It is identity and belonging.
– Elevate apprenticeships and technical training to equal status with universities.
– Reward firms that train and retain; penalise those that offshore or automate without civic duty.
– Rebuild respect for skilled trades as national service: the carpenter, the nurse, the engineer are as vital to the republic as the barrister or banker.
– Every citizen should feel that their work contributes not just to a wage, but to a nation.

4. Break Corporate Capture
Unregulated monopolies are not capitalism. They are its collapse.
– Enforce modern anti-monopoly laws against predatory consolidation in tech, media, energy, and housing.
– Make tax avoidance economically impossible with aggressive enforcement and transparency.
– Impose civic levies on industries that prey on weakness: gambling, payday lending, exploitative platforms.
– Create a Domestic Contribution Index: ranking firms by local hiring, training, reinvestment. Public contracts go only to those who pass.

5. Build an Ownership Society
Citizens must not just work in the economy. They must own part of it.
– Expand co-operatives, employee trusts, and mutuals with tax and procurement incentives.
– Tie public contracts to civic ownership standards: shared equity, worker voice, democratic governance.
– Make pensions transparent: citizens must know whether their savings build their nation or hollow it out.
– Establish national wealth funds that return profits to citizens, not just investors.
– A true liberal economy spreads ownership, because what you own, you defend.

No nation can defend itself on an empty stomach or a hollowed-out base. A shield made of paper laws will not stand if the economy beneath it is brittle, dependent, and demoralised. Without strength in production, sovereignty, and ownership, liberty is left balancing on debt and drift.

This is why the Forge follows the Lock. Once rules are secured, the next task is to ensure the nation has the tools to endure.

Work is not just a means to survive. It is how citizens take pride, learn discipline, and anchor themselves in the story of their country. Ownership is not just wealth, it is belonging.

A society where citizens neither own nor shape their economy becomes brittle, dependent, and easy prey for wolves who promise strength. The fascist offers national pride. The corporatist offers convenience. The accelerationist offers fire. All thrive in a nation where people feel the system is not theirs.

The forge tempers fire into steel. So must a nation temper ambition into dignity. For when people have a stake, they stay. They care. They stand guard. And only then can liberty last.

A strong economy gives us the means to choose our partners. The Forge shapes the tools, the Gate decides who we trade them with, and on what terms.

Third Pillar – The Gate

Trade & Strategic Independence

Trade is not neutral. It is a gate: open to friends, barred to foes. Leave it unguarded, and sovereignty slips quietly into foreign hands. Trade must be covenant, not concession. A tool that strengthens the home, not sells its keys.

For decades Britain treated trade as arithmetic, measured in tariffs and spreadsheets. We opened our markets without asking: who benefits? Who controls the chains? Who owns the infrastructure when the deal is done? The result was dependence dressed as prosperity, ports sold, utilities privatised, supply chains captured by rivals.

Mainstream liberalism clung to a fantasy: that openness

was always strength, that interdependence guaranteed peace, that the invisible hand would self-correct imbalance. It did not. Authoritarian regimes flooded our markets, bought our universities, acquired our utilities, and used our openness as a weapon. This was not trade. It was naivety masquerading as principle.

The Sheepdog Liberalism view is different. We do not reject commerce. But we reject servitude disguised as cooperation. Trade is a tool. Used wisely, it makes Britain freer, stronger, more secure. Used recklessly, it hollows us out and invites the wolves to feed.

The Four Bars of the Gate

1. **Values-Based Alliances**
   Trade is trust made tangible.
   – Deepen trade with liberal democracies; Canada, Japan, Australia, South Korea, Europe.
   – Embed democratic conditionality: transparency, labour rights, judicial independence.
   – Exclude regimes that weaponise supply chains or crush civic rights.

2. **Reciprocity, Not Reliance**
   Dependence is not partnership. It is leash and collar.
   – Conduct national dependency audits in critical inputs: minerals, energy, food, semiconductors, data.
   – Diversify and "friend-shore" supply chains with trusted allies.
   – Ban the sale of critical infrastructure to hostile or authoritarian states.

3. **Secure What We Need. Offer What We Excel At.**
   Trade should be symbiotic, not extractive.
   – Secure long-term access to rare earths, lithium, medical precursors, food security inputs.
   – Offer high-trust exports: green technology, education, secure digital infrastructure.
   – Treat Britain's civic reputation and institutions as export assets, not just its commodities.

4. **Defensive Measures & Sovereign Negotiation**

A gate is useless if it swings for everyone.
– Impose tariffs on hostile regimes that dump goods with forced labour or state subsidies.
– Prohibit authoritarian sovereign wealth funds from acquiring strategic assets.
– Create a Strategic Trade Corps: in-house negotiators accountable to Parliament, not consultants.
– Require parliamentary ratification for major trade deals with a civic impact test: not just GDP, but sovereignty.

Trade is not just about prices, it is about power. A nation that cannot choose its partners freely or defend its industries, is not sovereign. Britain's openness has too often meant exposure, its interdependence a mask for vulnerability.

This is why the Gate follows the Forge. Strength forged at home must be protected by wise exchange abroad. A pasture well tended still needs a gate that dictates who enters, and on what terms.

Globalisation promised that markets would soften tyrannies. Instead, it armed them. When democracies traded without condition, they did not export freedom, they imported fragility.

A sheepdog does not throw the gate open to the wolf and hope kindness will tame it. He chooses carefully who enters the field. He tests trust, and he bars those who would devour. Trade is not diplomacy by other means. It is self-governance, expressed through supply chains.

The cheapest deal is often the most expensive. The true measure of trade is not margin, but sovereignty.

The flock thrives, not by selling everything, but by choosing well. Yet a Gate means little if no one stands watch from the Tower above, and so the next defence must rise.

Fourth Pillar – The Tower

National Security & Civic Sovereignty

A nation that cannot defend itself cannot protect its values. Security is not paranoia. It is protection. It is the quiet strength that makes liberalism possible. Peace, prosperity, and pluralism are not natural states. They are built and guarded.

For too long, Britain has treated defence as an afterthought, even an embarrassment. Readiness was cast as regressive, vigilance as paranoia. We told ourselves goodwill was strategy, alliances a substitute for sovereignty. The result: hollowed forces, neglected logistics, infrastructure vulnerable to sabotage. Wolves do not wait for permission. They test for weakness.

The Sheepdog Liberalism view of defence is not militaristic. It is moral. We build strength not to conquer, but to guard. Because what we guard is fragile: speech, conscience, dissent, pluralism, peace. Security is not dominance. It is dignity with teeth.

The Four Towers of Security

1. Rebuild the Armed Forces for the 21st Century

Deterrence is not noise. It is readiness made visible.

– Increase funding for training, retention, and credible deterrence.
– Invest in logistics, cyber, and rapid deployment units.
– Build forces that can serve at home as well as abroad: disaster relief, infrastructure protection, emergencies.

2. Defend Critical Infrastructure

You cannot defend what you cannot secure.

– Protect defence-critical assets: bases, ports, communications, manufacturing.
– Establish rapid powers to nationalise or reclaim assets in crisis.
– Conduct resilience audits for sabotage, infiltration, and wartime continuity.

3. Secure Supply for War & Peace

Security cannot arrive on a container ship.

– Localise and diversify supply chains for essentials: food, fuel, medicine, munitions.
– Establish strategic reserves of critical inputs to survive blockade or disruption.
– Rebuild domestic capacity for defence components: semiconductors, satellites, advanced batteries.

4. **Civic Spirit of Defence**
   Defence is not just hardware. It is a habit of care.
   – Expand national service into cyber, infrastructure, and resilience roles.
   – Embed defence literacy in schools: not propaganda, but clarity on what liberal societies must guard.
   – Honour all service; military, civic, or emergency, as part of a covenant of protection.

Strength cannot be outsourced. A republic that cannot defend its food, fuel, code, or borders cannot defend its freedom for long. Britain's habit of outsourcing resilience has left it fragile.

This is why the Tower rises after the Gate. Even wise trade means little if no one is watching from above. A pasture with gates but no watchtower invites predators to gather unseen.

We do not arm ourselves because we crave conflict. We do so because what we've built is rare: the right to speak freely, to vote without fear, to worship or not, to live without a boot at the door. These are not universal conditions. They are fragile victories.

The sheepdog does not stand watch to dominate the world, but to ensure the world cannot dominate the flock. Security is not paranoia. It is vigilance turned outward, so liberty within can breathe.

Security alone can make a country rigid and fearful. The Tower must connect to the Bridge, so we can cross to allies, share our values, and meet the world on our own terms.

Fifth Pillar – The Bridge

Foreign Policy: Humility, Alliances & Liberal Realism

You don't spread liberalism with missiles. You prove it works.

For too long, Britain acted as though its role in the world was ordained as moral compass, liberal exporter, global steward. But confidence became performance. Summit speeches replaced stability. Military missions substituted for moral clarity. And while we looked outward, our civic core eroded at home.

The Sheepdog Liberalism view is different. We do not retreat from the world, but we do not posture either. We lead not through arrogance, but through example. We do not isolate, but align humbly with those who share our values and are willing to prove them in practice.

Foreign policy must be realist in tone, liberal in aim, civic in foundation. It begins not with dominance, but with restraint. Not with sentiment, but with structure. And it only acts abroad once the house is in order.

The Four Beams of the Bridge

1. **Credibility Before Command**
   You cannot project what you haven't protected.
   – Rebuild democratic institutions, civic trust, and national competence at home before claiming global leadership.
   – Stop lecturing nations on values we no longer uphold domestically.
   – Make civic renewal Britain's first act of diplomacy.

2. **Values-Based Alliances**
   The sheepdog chooses its pack with care.
   – Deepen alliances with democracies that share civic resilience: Europe, Canada, Australia, Japan, South Korea.
   – Support coalitions around digital sovereignty, anti-corruption, civic education, democratic infrastructure.
   – Build a Civic Compact Index: measure potential allies not just by GDP, but by civic performance.

3. **Aid With Strategic Purpose**
   Aid should be a scaffold, not a leash.
   – Prioritise democratic capacity-building: elections, civic education, watchdog institutions, free media.
   – Support fragile states against authoritarian influence: disinformation, cyber-espionage, corrupt investment.
   – Offer Aid-for-Sovereignty frameworks: infrastructure or security support in return for civic reform.

4. **Digital Statecraft**
   The new frontlines are written in code.
   – Lead a Civic Tech Alliance: develop ethical AI, open-source civic infrastructure, and public-interest platforms with democratic partners.
   – Pressure major tech firms to harden algorithms against foreign influence and extremist propaganda.
   – Build offensive and defensive cyber capacity, not just military but civic: digital literacy, misinformation countermeasures, platform accountability.

A country that cannot prove its model at home cannot preach it abroad. Britain's foreign policy drifted into contradiction: interventions without legitimacy, alliances without reciprocity, values without proof.

This is why the Bridge must follow the Tower. A watchtower without connection is isolation. A bridge without credibility is theatre. Only when the home is guarded can alliances carry real weight.

We do not need to preach. We need to be peers; strong at home, strategic abroad, trusted when we speak. Liberalism thrives when it is lived, not sold. Influence radiates from competence, not crusades.

The sheepdog does not bark across the valley to prove his courage. He stands firm in his own field, and then chooses carefully which allies to guard beside.

But not every crossing is for us to make. The Bridge goes out to others, the Door decides who comes in, and how they join the home we guard.

Sixth Pillar – The Door

Immigration & Integration: Borders with Purpose, Values with Strength

A nation without a border is not a sanctuary. It is awaiting collapse.

A home is not a fortress. But it is not a hallway, either. It has a door, and doors must have locks.

Immigration, handled wisely, is a gift. It brings energy,

renewal, and skill. But a gift without structure becomes disorder. When disorder spreads, compassion curdles into backlash, and liberalism collapses into fear.

Britain welcomed millions, but without clarity or cohesion. Integration was assumed, borders blurred, trust eroded. Liberal naivety mistook openness for strength, tolerance for indifference. It produced illiberal consequences while strongmen offered simple answers. Many listened.

The Sheepdog Liberalism view is different. We believe in immigration, but as structure, not spectacle. As contribution, not chaos. A sheepdog society guards its border not to exclude, but to ensure that those who cross it can fully belong.

The Four Hinges of the Door

1. **Rules-Based Entry**
   Without rules, welcome becomes weakness.
   – Distinguish clearly between legal and illegal entry.
   – Establish pre-entry processing centres abroad to vet asylum claims before Channel crossings.
   – Swiftly return those who enter illegally, while expanding lawful routes based on national need.

2. **Integration as Covenant**
   To join the flock is to share in its duties.
   – Require civic education for newcomers: rule of law, rights, gender equality, freedom of speech, civic responsibility.
   – Mandate English proficiency for long-term residency.
   – Introduce a Civic Service Pathway: newcomers contribute through service in healthcare, infrastructure, or education as part of integration.

3. **Protect the Public Realm**
   Diversity without duty is fragility.
   – Audit foreign funding of religious, cultural, and academic institutions.
   – Ban authoritarian-linked funding from schools, universities, mosques, and media.
   – Ensure public funds support only those institutions that affirm constitutional liberal values.

4. **Pathways to Belonging**
   The end of the journey is not entry, but belonging.
   – Provide fair, timely routes to citizenship for those who contribute and integrate.
   – Celebrate new citizens through public ceremonies that honour service and commitment, not just paperwork.
   – Create a National Integration Compact: equal rights, equal duties, equal pride.

A liberal state that cannot manage its border will not remain liberal for long. When immigration is unmanaged, resentment grows, cohesion fractures, and wolves rise. When it is principled, structured, and reciprocal, it strengthens the nation and renews its civic core.

This is why the Door follows the Bridge. No alliance abroad can compensate for collapse at home. A home is only as strong as those who live within it, and doors exist not to shut out the world, but to admit those ready to share in its defence.

Integration does not happen by accident. It happens by design: through language, service, and shared expectation. Generosity without judgment is not kindness. It is surrender.

The sheepdog does not throw open the gate to all who pass. He lets in those ready to live by the flock's rules, and bars those who would divide or devour. Immigration done right is not a threat to liberalism. It is one of its renewals.

A home is only as strong as those who live in it. Once the Door opens, the Root must grow, grounding every citizen in shared knowledge, skills, and civic purpose.

Seventh Pillar – The Root

Education & Human Development: Building Citizens, Not Just Workers

A liberal society survives only if it can reproduce itself. A tree without roots topples in the storm; a nation without civic formation drifts until it collapses. Education is not just preparation for work; it is the passing on of identity, discipline, and duty.

For decades, Britain's education system has been hollowed out. Once a ladder of opportunity and a pillar of shared culture, it became fragmented, ideological, overstretched. Civic purpose faded. Mental health declined. Too many young people left school unsure where they belonged, or what their country expected of them.

We don't just face a skills gap. We face a soul gap. Liberalism forgot that education is not only about performance, but about reproduction of values. We replaced civic duty with credentials, formation with output. The result: a generation fluent in exams but adrift in meaning; connected online but unrooted in life.

The Sheepdog Liberalism view is different. Education is civilisation work. It forms citizens, not just workers. It shapes guardians, not just consumers. It passes on a country worth defending.

The Six Roots of Education

1. **Civic Formation**
   Freedom must be taught, or it is lost.
   – Embed civic education at every level: institutions, rule of law, pluralism, Britain's constitutional story.
   – Teach what students inherit, not as propaganda, but as preparation.
   – Restore philosophy, ethics and politics to the core.

2. **Mental Resilience**
   An anxious mind cannot guard a free society.
   – Place trained mental-health professionals in every school.
   – Reform digital use: phones out of classrooms; invest in distraction-free tools.
   – Launch national digital-wellbeing literacy for families (how platforms work; how to reclaim attention).

3. **Free Minds, Not Fractured Ones**
   An education system captured is an education system wasted.
   – Mandate transparency in external content; bar ideological monopolies.
   – Protect academic freedom while confronting institutional conformity.

– Restore discipline and focus: classrooms of order, respect and moral seriousness.

4. **Nutrition & Capacity**
Hungry children do not learn; distracted children do not stand guard.
– Universal access to nutritious school meals (breakfast, lunch, after-school).
– Teach food literacy: cooking, growing, nutrition science.
– Design calm, focused learning environments, especially for disadvantaged pupils.

5. **Mentorship & Human Development**
Citizens are not mass-produced. They are cultivated.
– Anchor every school with trusted mentors drawn from veterans, teachers, and civic leaders to guide students in duty and discipline.
– Build cross-age mentoring and local service as standard practice.
– Tie schools to place: councils, civil society, community projects.

6. **Higher Education – Purpose Over Prestige**
Universities must serve truth, country and the common good, not dependency or vanity metrics.
– End dependency on authoritarian-linked income (student flows, grants, endowments) that compromise academic freedom.
– Prohibit partnerships with regimes that reject liberal values or suppress academic freedom; audit and bar foreign state-linked funding that undermines neutrality or institutional independence.
– Replace lost revenue with domestic civic investment targeted at high-impact disciplines, open research, and national capability (STEM, teacher training, healthcare, security, civic tech).
– Parity of esteem: put universities, apprenticeships, technical routes and the Civic Year (see Pillar Eight) on equal civic footing.
– Public mission compacts: link university funding to service (mentoring, local clinics, legal aid, civic tech labs) so campuses are engines of national renewal, not islands of prestige.

No society survives if it fails to form its young. Skills matter, but formation matters more. Without civic education, discipline and resilience, liberty rots from within; without independent, mission-driven universities, the nation forfeits truth and capacity to outside power.

This is why the Root follows the Door. A home that admits newcomers must also provide deep roots for them and for the native-born, or everyone drifts. Only when roots grow deep can branches grow strong.

A society that treats education as a commodity raises consumers. A society that treats education as civic work raises citizens. Liberalism survives only if it reproduces itself in duty, knowledge, and confidence.

The sheepdog does not raise pups by accident. He trains them patiently, in vigilance, discipline and care. So too must a republic raise each new generation not to be passive, but to be guardians.

But Roots alone do not teach service. From the soil of education, the Call must rise, inviting every young citizen to serve, contribute, and stand for something greater than themselves.

Eighth Pillar – The Call

The Civic Year: A National Rite of Passage

A free society cannot endure unless it teaches its people how to be free. Rights without rites are rootless; pride without service is shallow. We have raised generations with entitlements, but not with obligations. And the result is a society educated but unanchored, connected but unrooted, present but disengaged.

Where once there were transitions; school to work, boy to man, citizen to contributor, there is now only drift. The institutions that embedded responsibility – family, faith, service, military, civil society – have thinned or fractured. Too many young people enter adulthood anxious, isolated, and uncertain of where they belong.

The Sheepdog Liberalism view is different. We do not believe in manufactured patriotism or empty loyalty. We believe in earned pride. And pride comes from doing something real, with and for others.

The Five Rites of the Civic Year

1. **Pathways of Service**
   Duty should meet every citizen at the threshold of adulthood.
   – Every young person completes a 12-month Civic Year after leaving school or college at 18.
   – Choice of service streams: defence, infrastructure, healthcare, education, disaster response, digital/civic tech, local democracy.
   – No one is left without a path: each stream combines work experience, civic learning, and reflection.

2. **Training, Pay & Purpose**
   Service must sustain, not impoverish.
   – All participants receive a living stipend and training allowance.
   – Service placements are embedded within existing institutions or new mission-led teams.
   – Each year includes shared civic training: constitutional rights, crisis response, financial literacy, teamwork.

3. **Transition Support**
   The Civic Year should end with a bridge, not a void.
   – Completion earns a Civic Service Certificate.
   – Graduates receive tuition credits, apprenticeship vouchers, or job placement pipelines.
   – Mentorship built in: graduates either mentor younger students or are matched with senior mentors in chosen fields.

4. **Shared Objectives**
   The Civic Year is not just charity work. It is nation-building.
   – Rebuild civic culture across class and region.
   – Fill skill gaps in care, infrastructure, resilience.
   – Reconnect citizens to institutions as lived communities, not distant bureaucracies.
   – Seed leadership from the bottom up.

5. **Earned Belonging**
   You cannot love a country that never asked anything of you. And you cannot defend a society that never showed you where you belong.
   – Service ties rights to duties, teaching that liberty is not free.
   – Pride comes not from flag-waving, but from contribution.

– The Civic Year is not conscription. It is orientation: an invitation into citizenship.

No nation survives on freedom alone. It survives on preparation. Without shared rites of passage, liberal societies fray into atomisation and mistrust. The Civic Year gives every young citizen a moment of common duty, a foundation on which difference can rest.

This is why the Call follows the Root. Education plants knowledge and discipline, but only service binds them to a greater purpose. Roots grow deep, but the Call makes them stand tall.

A country that asks nothing will be loved lightly and defended poorly. A country that calls its young to serve earns loyalty that lasts a lifetime.

The sheepdog does not raise pups for leisure. He raises them for watchfulness, courage, and care. So too must a republic shape its guardians; not by force, but by invitation, pride, and duty shared.

Because liberal democracy is not inherited. It is rebuilt, by each generation, with intention.

Service strengthens the ties between people and state. The Call gives way to the Bond – a covenant of care, responsibility, and trust between citizen and society.

Ninth pillar – The Bond

The Social State: Care, Contribution & Services

A liberal state should feel like a guardrail, not a leash. It protects without smothering, empowers without patronising. Its purpose is not to manage lives, but to honour the conditions that make free life possible: health, housing, education, stability, and the chance to contribute.

For decades Britain drifted between two failures:
– A cold, bureaucratic neoliberalism that abandoned people to decline.

– A paternalistic statism that trapped people in dependency.

The result was cynicism and collapse. Services eroded, trust dissolved, belonging fractured. Wolves thrive where the bond between citizen and state is broken.

The Sheepdog Liberalism view is different. The state must protect dignity, reinforce responsibility, and invite every citizen to invest in the shared project. We do not want a bigger state. We want a better one: disciplined, trusted, and renewing itself through the loyalty it earns.

The Four Cornerstones of the Bond

1. **Health & Care**
   Care is not a cost. It is a moral signature.
   – Rebuild the NHS as a system of pride, not decline: fix digital systems, shift to preventative care, restore morale.
   – Treat social care as skilled labour: better pay, civic honour, community integration.
   – Build local support ecosystems that connect housing, health, and companionship.
   – Reform care homes on civic models with non-profit or capped-profit structures, transparent standards, and public accountability inspired by Denmark and Germany.
   – If NHS reforms prove effective, integrate long-term care within an NHS Care Branch to unite health, dignity, and oversight.

2. **Welfare as Contribution**
   Welfare should lift, not trap.
   – Simplify systems so support is fast, transparent, humane.
   – Make benefits conditional on contribution: civic service, mentorship, skill-building.
   – Introduce Civic Contribution Credits: unlock housing, training, or benefits through service and duty.

3. **Housing & Rootedness**
   A home is more than shelter. It is stability and belonging.
   – Expand citizen-led housing associations and empower local authorities.
   – Prioritise civic workers, veterans, mentors, and carers for access.

– Enforce quality and design standards: no concrete deserts, but rooted civic places.

4. **Services for Renewal**
   Every service should ask: what does this citizen become?
   – Education: not just exams, but civic literacy and formation.
   – Retraining: linked to real employer needs in AI, green tech, security.
   – Youth services: mentorship and leadership, not containment.
   – Public institutions: outcomes that rebuild civic pride, not outputs for bureaucracy.

The wolves feed on despair; addiction, loneliness, neglect. Where the state feels absent or predatory, people retreat into rage or resignation. Services are not luxuries. They are the scaffolding that makes liberty liveable.

This is why the Bond follows the Call. A citizen who has been asked to serve must also be supported. Service earns loyalty; loyalty is sustained by a state that proves itself worthy of trust.

A covenant must be two-sided. A country that demands contribution but offers nothing in return is unjust. A country that offers benefits with no duty corrodes itself.

The bond that protects a society is not built by teeth but by tending; by presence, fairness, and care. It binds citizens to one another so that none are left to drift alone. The bond is not soft. It is structure, scaffolding, trust made real.

A bond without direction can still drift. The Compass is what keeps the Bond true, guiding our institutions with integrity and earning the trust they claim.

Tenth Pillar – The Compass

Democratic Renewal & Institutional Trust

A free society cannot sail without a compass. Without direction, even strong institutions drift into capture and decay. Liberalism does not survive on goodwill alone. It survives on hard limits:

boundaries that bind power, and trust that binds citizens to the system.

Today Britain's democracy suffers not from a coup, but from erosion. Turnout is low. Lobbyists whisper louder than citizens. Parties chase headlines instead of horizons. The people are told to vote, and so they do, but the link between voice and result has frayed. This is how democracies fall: not with tanks, but with shrugs.

The Sheepdog Liberalism view is not cynical. It is disciplined. We do not tear down the system. We make it worthy again.

The Five Points of the Compass

1. **Time & Accountability**
   Government must look beyond headlines, but never beyond scrutiny.
   – Extend parliamentary terms from 5 to 10 years to allow deep reform.
   – At mid-point, hold a National Civic Review: independent oversight, public debate, measurable performance.
   – If Parliament loses two-thirds confidence, government falls. Accountability without short-termism.

2. **Voice & Representation**
   Elections should reflect the people, not just the parties.
   – Replace First-Past-the-Post with Single Transferable Vote (STV) to reduce wasted ballots.
   – Pilot Civic STV: ballots list candidate records of service and contribution.
   – Provide neutral voter guides and non-partisan ballot designs that elevate values above logos.

3. **A Civic Senate**
   The second chamber must be duty, not patronage.
   – Replace the unelected House of Lords with a Civic Senate.
   – Members drawn from service: health, armed forces, education, civil society, justice.
   – One single non-renewable term, selected by independent civic commissions.
   – Purpose: scrutiny, grounding, review, not partisan war.

4. Integrity & Transparency

Democracy dies in darkness, but thrives in daylight.
– Create a mandatory national lobbying register, covering source, target, and aim.
– Cap donations, enforce real-time disclosure, and ban all foreign political funding.
– Prohibit foreign state ownership of UK media and political infrastructure.
– Audit think tanks and universities for covert influence.

5. Ritual & Belief

Voting should feel like duty, not drudgery.
– Establish a national Voting Day holiday.
– Automatic registration at schools, GP surgeries, post offices.
– Ensure modern, accessible voting: early ballots, local access, transparent technology.
– Restore dignity to the ballot: participation as a civic rite, not an afterthought.

Democracy does not collapse in an instant. It dissolves quietly, as people stop believing their voice counts. The wolves thrive on that cynicism, selling rage in place of reform.

This is why the Compass follows the Bond. A state that provides care without direction becomes a cradle that drifts. A bond must be guided by a compass, pointing citizens and institutions toward a common horizon.

Liberty without limits is fragility. Power without trust is corruption. A true democracy asks not only for votes, but for vigilance.

The compass that guards a free society is not command but conscience. It measures drift before decline, checks the wind, and keeps our course aligned with principle. It does not dictate direction, but keeps the journey true.

Even with direction, a nation frays if it forgets its story. The Compass points the way, but the Fabric holds us together, stitching belonging across difference.

***

Eleventh Pillar – The Fabric

Culture & Belonging: A Nation Worth Coming Home To

You cannot defend a country you do not believe is yours. A flag without fabric is just cloth; a nation without culture is just land. Belonging is the thread that makes liberty durable.

Modern liberalism tried to sidestep culture. It outsourced meaning to markets, reduced identity to lifestyle, treated history as embarrassment. The result was predictable: citizens fled to nostalgia, tribalism, or resentment. The far right offered roots. The far left offered rupture. Liberalism stood shrinking, caught between shame and denial.

The Sheepdog Liberalism view is different. We do not impose a singular identity. We weave a shared fabric, stitched from difference but bound by duty. Culture is not decoration. It is the hearth around which liberty gathers, the inheritance that makes sacrifice meaningful.

The Four Threads of Belonging

1. **Integration With Expectation**
   Diversity without duty frays the weave.
   – Strengthen citizenship: real civic training, service, and English fluency.
   – Launch a National Integration Agreement: full rights matched with law, service, language.
   – Create civic mentorships for newcomers, pairing them with teachers, veterans, carers, and local leaders.

2. **Historical & Civic Literacy**
   A people without memory is a people without guardrails.
   – Embed Britain's civic history into schools: not whitewashed, not ashamed, but honest.
   – Teach the development of liberal democracy: rights, duties, the struggle to get here.
   – Restore philosophy and ethics to education so citizens can reason through conflict.

3. **Shared Story in Public Space**
   Public places are not neutral. They tell a nation what it values.

- Restore and protect civic architecture, monuments, and art reflecting sacrifice and solidarity.
- Fund museums, libraries, and local institutions, especially in abandoned towns.
- Invest in public rituals and town-based cultural grants that celebrate pluralism and pride.

4. Localism as Cultural Renewal

Culture is lived locally, not just displayed nationally.

- Support local media and regional broadcasting.
- Encourage interfaith and inter-community gatherings.
- Back clubs, festivals, football pitches, and community halls as the true commons of trust.

Liberal societies collapse not just from invasion, but from indifference. When citizens no longer feel they share a story, they stop defending it. Wolves whisper rage and shame where no fabric holds.

This is why the Fabric follows the Compass. Institutions can point the way, but without a shared culture the nation cannot move together. A compass without fabric is a tool without a sail.

A nation is not a hotel. It is an inheritance, paid for in sacrifice, sustained by duty, handed on with care.

Belonging in a free society does not mean uniformity. It means seriousness about what we hold in common, and the will to defend it together. Unity is not sameness, but shared conviction held in common purpose.

And a Fabric without structure will fold under strain. Its Spine is justice and order, the framework that keeps freedom standing.

Twelfth Pillar – The Spine

Justice & Order: The Moral Spine of a Free Society

Without safety, freedom is a rumour. A society that cannot protect its people will not remain liberal for long. The wolves rise when justice fails, promising order without liberty, vengeance without law.

For decades, Britain swung between neglect and overreach.

VOLUME III: THE SHIELD

Crime was politicised, policing target-driven, prisons overcrowded yet ineffective, victims forgotten. Rehabilitation was reduced to rhetoric, prevention an afterthought. Authoritarian crackdowns failed. Performative leniency failed. The result was distrust, and drift.

The Sheepdog Liberalism view is different. Justice must be firm, fast, and fair. It must restrain the guilty, protect the innocent, and restore those who can return. For order without mercy is tyranny and mercy without order is collapse.

The Four weights of justice

1. **Policing for Presence & Trust**
   Guardianship begins on the ground.
   – Fund visible, community-based policing, officers who know their streets.
   – Equip forces with modern forensics, bodycams, and case systems for speed and integrity.
   – End target-chasing incentives; reward responsiveness, resolution, and trust.

2. **Civic Correction & Rehabilitation**
   Discipline without redemption is waste.
   – Establish Civic Service Corps pathways as alternatives for first-time and youth offenders.
   – Completion seals records, builds skills, opens jobs.
   – Not leniency, but structured restitution, discipline, and contribution.

3. **Transparency & Accountability**
   Justice must be seen to be believed.
   – Independent investigations into systemic failures: grooming gangs, institutional abuse.
   – Publish anonymised local crime data and justice system metrics.
   – Enforce equal sentencing standards to restore fairness.

4. **Justice That Rebuilds**
   Punishment is not the end; return is the goal.
   – Expand restorative justice where victims choose it.
   – Create diversion courts for addiction and mental illness, with mandatory treatment.

– Equip prisons for rehabilitation: literacy, vocational training, structured re-entry.

Justice is the test of trust. If citizens believe crime will be ignored or punished unfairly, they retreat into rage or resignation. Wolves thrive on that collapse, offering security without liberty.

This is why the Spine comes last. A nation can have roots, a compass, even fabric, but without a spine it cannot stand.

Justice is not vengeance. It is the backbone that keeps liberty upright. We do not bite for pleasure; we act to protect what is ours. Strength must be joined with mercy, and order must give security without cruelty.

The Spine of a free nation is discipline with purpose, strength with mercy, and justice with order. Only through these can law be not only enforced, but believed in.

Let the Sheepdog Lead

A Closing Call for the Great Repair

We live in a country where trust is dissolving: In government, in the system, in one another. Not because people hate Britain, but because they were promised a deal: Work hard. Play fair. Do your bit.

And in return, you'd have a home, a future, a place in the story.

That deal was broken. By leaders chasing headlines, not legacy; by markets without mission; by institutions that lost their spine and their soul.

When trust collapses, the wolves move in, selling fear and rage, tearing at what's left of the centre.

The 12 Pillars of the Shield are our answer.

They are not nostalgia. They are not softness. They are not surrender. They are a plan to guard liberty with strength, and to build strength with purpose.

They mean:

- Markets that serve the nation.
- Ownership as belonging.
- Borders that are firm and fair.
- A justice system that is strong and just.
- A democracy worth trusting.
- National service that builds character.
- Communities rooted in real places, with real stakes.

This is not ideology for ideology's sake. It is about giving people real control. Over their homes, their work, their communities, their future.

We will defend that not with anger, not with tribalism, but with duty, clarity, and resolve.

Because liberalism without strength gets eaten.

And strength without liberalism eats everything.

This is not revolution. This is repair.

We do not seek power for power's sake. We seek it to serve, to protect, to build.

Let the wolves circle.

Let the sheepdog lead.

The Wider Pasture

But the wolves do not circle Britain alone. They circle every open society. They test every pasture where liberty grazes, every nation where power is checked by principle, every people who dare to live as citizens instead of subjects.

The forms differ; corruption in one land, sectarianism in another, corporate predation in a third, but the pattern is the same. Liberal nations are fragile because they depend not on force, but on belief: belief in rules, restraint, institutions, and in one another. When that belief falters, the wolves find their way in.

Sheepdog Liberalism is written here for Britain, but it is not a British ideology. It is a civic one. The parables of guardrails, gates, and teeth belong to any free people. A sheepdog is not bound by soil or flag. He is bound by duty: to protect the flock, to restrain himself, to ensure the home endures.

Every nation that still claims liberty must decide: will it guard its flock with vigilance and structure, or drift into spectacle and decay? Wolves are patient. They have already devoured pastures where no sheepdog stood and they will devour more.

The call is not for Britain alone. It is for democracies across the world to grow teeth, to build fences, to renew trust, and to stand together as guardians of their own freedom. Sheepdog Liberalism is a shield that any free people can carry. If we do not carry it, we will carry chains instead.

Peace returned, but it carried memory. The flock understood the cost of vigilance and the fragility of all they kept. The sheepdogs moved quietly along the boundaries, teaching those who followed that peace is never given, only maintained.

Freedom, they knew, would endure only through courage, discipline, and the daily care of those who stand watch.

The Civic Contract

The Twelve Pillars show us what can be touched and measured: reforms of law, power, industry, and place. Yet a nation is held together by more than its visible parts. It could be argued that the most important repair of all is not tangible but invisible. It is the quiet trust between citizens, and the covenant that binds them to their country. This is the civic contract, and without it every pillar will rest on sand

Section 1 – What Holds a Nation Together

A nation is not held together by its borders, by the text of its laws, or by the symbols on its coins. These things matter, but they are scaffolds. They are hollow if nothing lives inside them.

What holds a nation together is belief.

Not the shallow kind performed for cameras or paraded

on command, but the kind people live without needing to announce. The quiet conviction that binds you not only to the place where you live, but to the millions of others who share it with you, known and unknown, through a shared understanding of what you owe one another.

For a time, Britain had this. Not as an official doctrine or conscious plan, but as an assumption passed down like an accent. That freedom was precious. That fairness mattered. That each generation owed the next something better than it had received. That being a citizen was not simply about being served, but about serving in return. We did not need to talk about a civic contract because we were living inside it.

Now, we are not.

The break did not arrive in a single crisis. It came slowly, through a hundred quiet withdrawals: responsibility handed off to someone else, contribution replaced with complaint, the slow turning of *us* into *them*. Where citizenship once meant participation, it has been reduced to a login page, a tax bracket, a right to object without any urge to help. The public realm has come to feel less like a shared home and more like a service counter. A place you visit only to make a demand.

But no society can endure on rights alone. Rights are not self-sustaining; they rest on trust, and trust rests on participation. You cannot automate belonging. You cannot manufacture purpose. And you cannot keep a society free if no one feels responsible for keeping it whole. Yet we have built a culture in which citizens are encouraged to live as if they are alone. Drifting between consumption and outrage, unmoored from place, disconnected from duty, taught to distrust institutions and each other; we should not be surprised when this leaves people anxious, alienated, or angry.

This is what happens when the invisible threads of civic life – obligation, neighbourliness, earned pride – are left to fray. The wolves do not need to cut them. They only wait, knowing that if we let the strands wear thin enough, the whole fabric will give way on its own. And when that moment comes, they move in.

But what has been frayed can still be rewoven.

The soul of Britain is not gone. It waits – quiet, calloused, tired of false promises – for someone to speak to it with honesty.

To say: you are not only a consumer. You are not only a voter. You are a citizen. And this place – this flawed, liberal, hard-won home – is yours to guard, yours to repair, yours to pass on.

No empire will step in to save it. No technology will patch it up. No strongman will protect it without exacting a price too steep to bear. It is us. Only us. That is what holds a nation together. And if we choose to remember that, the threads can be mended. Not easily. Not quickly. But enough to hold. Enough to stand. Enough to begin again.

Section 2 – The Forgotten Agreement

No law alone can bind a people together. Surveillance cannot create loyalty, taxation cannot inspire pride, and digital access cannot fabricate cohesion where it has been lost.

What holds a free nation together is not power or fear, but trust. Not naïve trust, but the earned, reciprocal kind that grows when citizens and their society recognise a shared stake in each other's wellbeing.

At its simplest, it is an unspoken pact: *I give because it gives to me. I serve because it protects me. I defend it because I belong.* This is the civic contract. It may not be written into constitutions, though it gives constitutions their strength. It may not be codified in law, though it allows laws to work. It lives in the spaces between institutions; in a handshake, in a vote honestly cast, in a street swept by someone who does not own the houses along it. It lives in the instinct to say, "This is my home, even if I did not build it, and I will act accordingly."

But this pact is not one-sided. In a healthy society, the state carries its own share of the bargain. If the citizen owes loyalty, service, and participation, the state owes fairness, competence, and protection. It must keep its promises with the same seriousness it asks of its people. It must guard the rights it proclaims, deliver the justice it demands, and steward the public realm it expects its citizens to maintain. When the state neglects these duties, it erodes the moral authority to ask for service in return. When citizens neglect theirs, the state's capacity to uphold the common good collapses. The fate of state and citizen is bound together; in weakness or in strength, they share the same end.

Britain once lived closer to this bond. Not perfectly, but enough. People knew their neighbours. They shared reference points and rituals. The nation, though flawed, still felt like theirs. They bore some duty to it, and it, in turn, owed something to them. When someone fell ill, soup appeared on the doorstep. When floods came, sandbags were filled without anyone asking who would be paid. When elections arrived, turnout was high, not because politicians inspired, but because the act of voting itself meant something.

It was never utopia. But it was *us*.

Much of that has faded, not through a single betrayal or disaster, but through slow neglect on both sides. The civic contract was not torn apart; it was left to rot. Today, many are citizens on paper but strangers in practice. Rights are well known, but responsibilities are often forgotten. We speak of freedom while retreating from the obligations that sustain it. We have more platforms to express ourselves than ever, yet fewer spaces where we act together on behalf of something greater than ourselves.

Into that vacuum, other forces rush in. Grievance becomes identity. Cynicism becomes culture. Politics becomes bloodsport; not because people hate each other, but because they have forgotten they are on the same side.

This is not a question of etiquette. It is a question of survival. Liberal democracy cannot function without citizens and a state who recognise they are bound to one another; not by force, not out of blind loyalty, but because they each see the other as indispensable. The civic contract is not nostalgia. It is the only antidote we know to the slow collapse of a free society. And without it, freedom will quietly dismantle itself.

Section 3 – Symptoms of a Broken Bond

The decline of civic life in Britain did not arrive with riots or revolutions. It came quietly, in the empty spaces where participation used to live; in town halls with chairs stacked in the corner, in ballots left unmarked, in streets where neighbours pass without recognition.

You can feel it even if you can't name it. A kind of atmospheric drift. The machinery of daily life still runs – trains arrive, bills get paid, debates are held – but something vital is missing. The thread that once tied people to each other and to the country they share, has grown thin.

Walk through a mid-sized town and the signs are everywhere. A library stands shuttered, its noticeboard still advertising events from years ago. The youth centre closed five summers past, without ceremony or protest. The park is overgrown, while a privately run gym two streets over thrives. Betting shops outnumber post offices. The pub doubles as a food bank. People still live there, but fewer feel they belong.

Turnout in elections falls year after year, until a handful of votes decide the future for thousands. Volunteering dwindles; there are fewer coaches, fewer scout leaders, fewer people willing to give the slow, steady hours that hold a community together. Among the young, loneliness is no longer an occasional pang but a chronic condition, described not in moments but in years.

Yet the most telling symptom is not hostility. It is withdrawal. People retreat into private worlds; their energy spent on personal survival or digital distraction. They stop showing up to parents' evenings. They no longer bother with local meetings. They feel invisible, and start behaving as though the place around them belongs to someone else.

And when this happens across an entire country, you don't get an explosion. You get drift, a slow detachment from the shared life of the nation. A society that functions but no longer believes.

That drift leaves a vacuum, and vacuums are quickly filled. Into it step those who promise belonging through division, meaning through rage, purpose through blame. The wolves do not sell solutions; they sell enemies. And when the bonds between citizens are thin enough, that is often all it takes.

Yet beneath the apathy and the anger lies something quieter and more human: the wish to matter. The desire to be part of a story worth continuing. That is what is truly lost when the civic bond frays; not only participation, but the shared belief that our efforts change anything at all. And it is that belief which must be restored first, if the rest is to follow.

***

Section 4 – From Entitlement to Honour

We live in an age where rights are spoken of loudly and responsibilities are barely whispered. In a liberal democracy, that imbalance is not just unsustainable, it is dangerous. Rights that are claimed without the willingness to sustain them grow brittle. They can be demanded, brandished, even weaponised. But they cannot endure.

Somewhere along the way, a quiet myth took root: that liberalism simply exists, that freedom is like the weather, it comes and goes without effort on our part. Citizenship became a status rather than a role, a matter of paperwork rather than participation. But freedom does not renew itself. It survives only because someone is willing to stand guard, to carry it forward, to repair what wears thin.

You are free because others defended that freedom. You have rights because someone before you believed they were worth protecting. You speak because a society was built that allows it.

Forget this, and one day you will reach for those freedoms and find they are no longer there.

In this climate, two false paths are offered. One is the path of the passive consumer; tuned out, scrolling through despair, treating the country like a broken vending machine. The other is the path of the radical; eager to burn it all down, convinced that collapse is the only cure. Both are dead ends.

Between them lies a third path: the civic citizen.

The civic citizen shows up. They critique, but they also contribute. They believe in their country enough to hold it accountable and help it heal. They do not wait for perfect leaders or flawless systems. They take responsibility for what is within their reach: a park cleaned, a vote cast, a neighbour helped, a voice raised not to rage, but to repair.

They understand something deeper: that while the nation owes them protection, justice, and opportunity, they also owe the nation their service, loyalty, and care. This is not about obedience. It is about stewardship, the act of caring for something because it matters and because you have a hand in its fate.

Honour is the measure here. Not the kind worn on medals, but the kind you carry within yourself. It comes from the knowledge that you have done your part; that you have helped build, defend, and improve something worth passing on. It is the quiet pride of belonging to a place you have served, of being able to say, *I stood my ground. I made my contribution.*

Entitlement weakens the bond between citizen and country. Honour strengthens it. Entitlement treats the nation as a service provider. Honour treats it as a shared inheritance. Entitlement asks, *what will you give me?* Honour asks, *what will we build together?*

And when enough people choose honour over entitlement, the civic contract ceases to be an abstract ideal and becomes the lived reality of the nation. That is the turning point. That is the foundation on which everything else in a free society rests.

Section 5 – Earned Belonging

Too many people today feel like strangers in their own country. For some, the nation feels like a hotel; a place they pass through, built and maintained by others, without any sense of ownership or obligation. For others, it feels like it was designed for someone else entirely, and they are merely guests. Part of that alienation is economic, but part of it is civic.

We have stopped giving people ways to earn their belonging. When you do not help build something, you rarely feel responsible for it. When you are not invited to contribute, you begin to distrust those who are in charge. And when your only connection to your nation comes through taxes, headlines, or grievances, the idea of pride in it begins to sound absurd.

In the past, belonging was not a label; it was the by-product of shared effort. You saw it in the village that rebuilt its hall after a fire, in the floodplain where neighbours worked side by side to keep the river back, in the street where people took turns caring for an ailing resident. No one needed to ask if they belonged; their belonging was in the work itself.

This is why civic responsibility matters. It is not simply about maintaining public spaces or delivering services. It is about giving every citizen the chance to place their hands on the foundations of the country and leave their mark there. When you have done that; when you have helped repair, protect, or improve something that others rely on, the nation is no longer an abstraction. It becomes yours.

Belonging earned in this way is different from inherited loyalty or symbolic patriotism. It is quieter, steadier, and far harder to shake. It endures across disagreements and outlasts political cycles because it is rooted in action, not in rhetoric. And when enough citizens feel this kind of belonging, the fabric of the nation becomes stronger than the forces that would pull it apart.

Section 6 – The Civic Dividend

In politics, the first question is almost always, *what will this cost?* But some of the most valuable returns a nation can earn cannot be measured in money. Trust, cohesion, dignity, and hope are not line items in a budget. They are the by-products of a society in which citizens take responsibility for what they share.

This is the civic dividend: the return we all receive when people see themselves as participants rather than passengers. It is not theoretical. It is the lift you feel when a place is cared for because those who live there believe it is theirs. It is the resilience of a community that can absorb a shock and recover because its people are already connected.

The absence of this dividend is visible in the crises we mislabel as purely economic or political. Loneliness, alienation, youth despair, and deep distrust in public institutions all have a common root: the loss of shared purpose. People are not disengaged because they have nothing to say; they are disengaged because no one is asking them to take part. The spaces where they once felt useful, from the parish hall to the building site, from the sports pitch to the local council chamber, have been allowed to fade.

When people are given visible ways to contribute, something shifts. It might be a library kept open because enough volunteers turned up, a neighbour helped through illness, a footpath repaired by residents, a planning decision shaped by those it affects. In each case, the action restores more than the object repaired; it restores the belief that individual effort can still change the collective outcome.

The effects are not just civic; they are personal. A growing body of research shows that purpose is not a luxury, it is a protective factor for mental and physical health. Loneliness is as lethal as obesity or smoking, and purpose is its most effective antidote. When people feel their presence matters, when their work is seen, when they can point to something tangible and say *I helped do that*, their lives take on a stability that no algorithm or subsidy can replicate.

Shared purpose also builds trust. Not because differences disappear, but because working side by side on something real forces us to see each other as partners rather than opponents. A repaired playground or revitalised high street becomes proof that cooperation is still possible, even in a divided age.

This is what the civic dividend offers: a society in which people trust one another enough to share the load, and value one another enough to keep showing up. In that kind of country, freedom feels real because it is reinforced by daily experience, not only printed in a constitution.

Section 7 – Conclusion: A Nation Worth Defending

You cannot automate cohesion.

You cannot outsource belief.

And you cannot defend what no one feels belongs to them.

If Britain is to endure as a liberal democracy not just in name, but in practice, then it must do more than protect freedoms on paper. It must make those freedoms felt in the daily lives of its people. That means rebuilding what has been lost: not just institutions, but relationships; not just policies, but trust; not just structures of governance, but the invisible architecture of responsibility.

The Civic Contract is that architecture. It is not enforced by law. It is sustained by culture. It does not require unanimity; it requires participation. It is not about perfect loyalty; it is about showing up. When that contract is strong, people stop asking if their country is worth saving. They already know, because they have helped build it. And that is the most powerful force in politics: ***a citizen who believes the nation is theirs.***

We do not pretend that a single policy will restore this. But we believe that every act of national renewal – every apprenticeship, every civic project, every act of local stewardship – is a thread, slowly weaving the fabric back together. This section has argued something simple, perhaps the most unfashionable political idea of all: that the citizen matters. That freedom is not defended by platitudes or sentiment, but by people who choose, again and again, to uphold it; not because they are told to, but because they believe in it.

This belief cannot be commanded. But it can be cultivated. It can be invited. It can be rewarded. And when it is, everything else becomes possible: a better economy; a stronger democracy; a culture with spine. None of these are delivered from above. They are forged in the quiet, daily work of citizens who see their freedom not as a gift, but as a responsibility.

We call this a Civic Contract. Others might call it trust. Whatever the name, it is the only thing that has ever held a free society together. And if we are to survive the century ahead, not merely as a functioning nation, but as something worth inheriting, then that contract must be renewed. By us. Now. Together.

The shield is not something to be wielded. It is to be lived. You. We, the people, are the shield of Britain.

Epilogue: The Watch Begins

Britain is ours. But if you do not act, it will not remain that way. I have placed my faith in the people of Britain because I know that, despite the apathy and the hardships that have worn you down, despite the wolves pressing at our gates, we are still a strong people. We carry a proud history forged in struggle, proven in triumph, and we will not bow to the wolves of chaos.

It is better to stand in defence of our liberty, structure, children, and the future they will inherit, than to kneel before the wolves at the gate. Our spirit is unyielding. I stand because Britain is worth fighting for. For the pride of what it means to be British, and the privilege it is to call this place our home. But I cannot stand alone.

I need you. Not in arms. Not in ranks beneath me. But beside me; shoulder to shoulder, pack to pack.

For only the people of Britain can save Britain, and only the people of Britain can decide its future. In a time when the wolves thrive on disconnection and apathy, the choice to belong, act, and claim responsibility becomes the most radical act of all.

I speak not only to liberals, but to all who consider themselves

British. To anyone who believes this country is still worth defending. What I ask is not loyalty to a party, but loyalty to each other: to a new evolution of liberalism. A liberalism with purpose. A liberalism that knows who it is. A movement that seeks not to manage decline, but to uplift the life and dignity of the citizen, not only out of duty, but out of respect. For the citizen is the foundation of the country. Not a pawn to be moved, not a metric of GDP to be played with, but the very fabric of Britain's future.

We will rebuild the civic flame. We will protect the vulnerable without surrendering our strength. We will teach our children that liberty is not inherited; it is earned, and it is guarded. There is still time to steer this nation from the brink; but not in silence, not in isolation, not "someday." Only together. Only now.

This is not faith offered blindly, but faith earned by the strength of our people. If you are reading this, you are already a part of it. You are no longer a spectator.

You are the watch.

Let the wolves be afraid.

The sheepdogs stand guard.

VOLUME IV: The Seal

The Constitutional Framework

The speech has ended. What follows is not rhetoric but record: the Seal of Sheepdog Liberalism. This constitution is not a vision, but the structure that preserves it. Where the Soul, the Siege, and the Shield spoke of philosophy, threat, and defence, the Seal sets down the rules that bind them together.

The Constitution for a United Kingdom

Adopted by the people in defence of liberty, duty, and justice

PREAMBLE

We, the people of the United Kingdom, establish this Constitution to guard liberty and to restrain power. For freedom without duty is fragile, and rights without responsibility are soon lost. The enemies of Liberalism lie not only beyond our borders but within our own divisions, when fear, greed, or corruption turn neighbour against neighbour. Therefore, we bind authority with law, tie liberty to service, and place watchmen over power itself. We pledge that government shall be of the people, by the people, for the people, in defence from the people, so that no citizen shall be enslaved by tyranny, deception, or neglect, and so that justice, duty, and belonging may endure for generations to come.

ARTICLE 1 - SUPREMACY, SOVEREIGNTY & FORM OF STATE

Section 1 - Supremacy of the Constitution

1. This Constitution is the supreme law of the United Kingdom.
2. Any law, regulation, or act of government inconsistent with this Constitution is void to the extent of inconsistency.
3. Courts are empowered to declare such inconsistency and provide effective remedies, including striking down legislation, issuing suspended declarations of invalidity, or requiring corrective action by Parliament.
4. No institution or individual is above the Constitution.

Section 2 - Sovereignty

1. Sovereignty resides in the people of the United Kingdom.
2. The people exercise sovereignty through their elected representatives, through referendums held under this Constitution, and through the civic duties required of all citizens.
3. No institution, whether legislative, executive, judicial, military, or otherwise, may claim authority except as granted by this Constitution.

Section 3 - Form of the State

1. The United Kingdom is a democratic republic and a union of nations, founded on equality, liberty, and the rule of law.
2. The Constitution guarantees the autonomy of its constituent nations and local governments within the framework of reserved and devolved powers.
3. The national capital shall be London; other institutions may be distributed across the nations by law.

Section 4 - Continuity of Law

1. All laws, regulations, and acts in force at the date of commencement of this Constitution shall remain valid unless clearly inconsistent with its provisions.
2. Within five years of commencement, Parliament shall review and align existing law with this Constitution.

ARTICLE 2 - THE HEAD OF STATE

Section 1 - Form of Office

1. The United Kingdom shall remain a constitutional monarchy, with the Crown as Head of State.
2. The Crown is purely ceremonial. All public powers of the monarchy are abolished, except those expressly delegated by this Constitution or statute to ministers accountable to Parliament.
3. No prerogative powers shall exist outside this Constitution and statute.

***

Section 2 - Duties of the Crown

1. The monarch shall:
    - Represent national unity at ceremonial events.
    - Formally appoint as Prime Minister the person designated by the House of Commons.
    - Promulgate laws duly enacted by Parliament.
    - Uphold and symbolically safeguard this Constitution.
2. All acts of the Crown require ministerial countersignature; ministers bear responsibility.

Section 3 - Assets and Revenues

1. All assets of the Crown are public property, held in trust for the people of the United Kingdom.
2. Members of the Royal Family shall receive civil allowances as determined by statute, subject to review by Parliament.
3. Over time, Parliament shall phase Crown assets and estates fully into public ownership.

Section 4 - Sunset Clause

1. Beginning twenty years after the commencement of this Constitution, Parliament shall convene a Constitutional Review to consider the continuation of the monarchy.
2. The monarchy may be abolished by:
    - A two-thirds vote in both Houses of Parliament; and
    - Approval by a majority of voters in a national referendum.
3. Upon abolition, all ceremonial and symbolic functions of the Crown shall pass to a non-executive President, elected or appointed as provided by amendment.
4. All assets, estates, and revenues of the Crown shall return to the people and the state. No property or privilege shall remain vested in a royal family or private heirs.

Section 5 - Transition to a Republic

- In the event of abolition, the President shall inherit no additional powers beyond those defined for the ceremonial Crown.
- All oaths of allegiance shall transfer from the Crown to the Constitution and the people.
- Parliament shall pass necessary statutes to effect orderly transition within one year of the referendum.

ARTICLE 3 - BILL OF RIGHTS & DUTIES

Section 1 - General Principles

1. The rights and freedoms set out in this Article belong to all persons within the United Kingdom.
2. These rights are directly enforceable in any court of law, and all public authorities must act compatibly with them.
3. Rights may only be limited by laws that are clear, general, pursue a legitimate aim, and are necessary and proportionate in a democratic society.
4. Rights may not be suspended except under the lawful derogation procedure set out in this Constitution.

Section 2 - Core Rights

Every person has the right to:

- Life and Security - protection of life and bodily integrity; prohibition of torture, inhuman or degrading treatment or punishment.
- Liberty - freedom from arbitrary arrest or detention; habeas corpus guaranteed.
- Due Process and Fair Trial - presumption of innocence, access to counsel, impartial tribunal, and trial within reasonable time.
- Privacy - respect for home, family, communications,

and data; surveillance only under law, necessity, proportionality, and independent judicial warrant.

- Expression and Press - freedom of speech, press, art, and information; protection for whistleblowers and journalists.
- Conscience, Religion, and Belief - freedom to hold or change beliefs and to practice or not practice religion.
- Assembly and Association - freedom of peaceful protest, association, and to form or join trade unions.
- Equality before the Law - equal protection without discrimination based on sex, race, religion, belief, disability, age, sexual orientation, or other status.
- Vote and Participation - the right to vote in free and fair elections, to stand for office, and to take part in civic processes.
- Education - right to access free primary and secondary education; higher education to be made progressively accessible.
- Property - right to own, inherit, and dispose of property; deprivation only in public interest with compensation.
- Remedy - right to an effective remedy before an independent court when rights are violated.

Section 3 - Modern Rights

1. Digital Rights - protection of personal data; right to online privacy; prohibition of mass surveillance without lawful basis.
2. Environmental Rights - right to a healthy, sustainable environment; duty of the state to protect nature and future generations.
3. Children's Rights - right of every child to protection, education, care, and participation consistent with their age and maturity.
4. Disability Rights - guarantee of equal access and reasonable accommodation for persons with disabilities.

Section 4 - Non-Derogable Rights

The following rights shall never be limited or suspended:

1. Right to life.
2. Freedom from torture or slavery.
3. Freedom from retroactive criminal punishment.
4. Recognition as a person before the law.

Section 5 - Remedies and Enforcement

1. Courts may grant declarations, injunctions, damages, or other effective remedies for violations.
2. Where legislation is incompatible with this Article, courts may strike down the provision or issue a suspended declaration of invalidity to allow corrective legislation.
3. Public interest litigation shall be permitted; standing rules must allow individuals, groups, or organisations to defend rights on behalf of affected persons.
4. Parliament shall establish and fund an independent Human Rights Commission to monitor and promote compliance.

Section 6 - Duties of Citizenship

1. Every citizen has duties of:
    - Participation in democratic life.
    - Defence of the civic order against corruption, misinformation, and authoritarianism.
    - Stewardship of public goods and the natural environment.
    - Honesty and good faith in civic participation.
2. These duties are directive principles of state policy, shaping law and education.

Section 7 - Mandatory Civic Year

1. Every citizen shall undertake a Civic Year of national service, normally between the ages of 18 and 25.
2. Service shall last no less than 9 months and no more than 12 months, as determined by statute.
3. Approved areas of service include:
    - Environmental restoration and climate resilience.
    - Education and tutoring support.
    - Healthcare and care work.
    - Engineering and digital infrastructure.
    - Emergency response, disaster relief, and civil protection.
    - Community renewal and local government projects.
    - Military and defence-related roles for those who choose them.
4. Citizens unable to participate in standard programmes due to disability, faith, or hardship shall be assigned equivalent alternative service.
5. Completion of the Civic Year is a precondition for full civic rights, including eligibility for election, senior public office, and receipt of state honours.
6. Citizens who refuse without lawful exemption shall face proportionate penalties, to be set by statute.
7. Immigrants applying for naturalisation shall complete a Civic Year as part of their integration; time served in approved service programmes prior to application may count toward this duty.
8. Parliament shall establish a National Civic Service Authority to organise placements, ensure fairness, and protect the dignity of all participants.

ARTICLE 4 - THE LEGISLATURE

Section 1 - Establishment

1. Legislative power is vested in a Parliament of two Houses: the House of Commons and the Civic Senate.

2. Parliament shall make laws for the peace, order, and good governance of the United Kingdom, subject always to this Constitution.
3. No House may suspend itself or extend its term except as expressly provided in this Constitution.

Section 2 - The House of Commons

1. Members of the Commons (MPs) shall be elected by Single Transferable Vote in multi-member constituencies.
2. The Commons shall be elected for a term of 10 years.
3. The Commons holds primacy in matters of confidence and public finance.
4. Qualifications for membership, incompatibilities of office, and disqualification grounds shall be determined by statute consistent with this Constitution.
5. The Commons shall elect its own Speaker, who presides impartially and represents the House before the Crown, Senate, and courts.

Section 3 - The Civic Senate

1. The Civic Senate replaces the House of Lords as the upper chamber of Parliament.
2. The Senate shall consist of 71 Senators.
3. Representation shall be allocated as follows:
    - England: 41 Senators.
    - Scotland: 15 Senators.
    - Wales: 10 Senators.
    - Northern Ireland: 5 Senators.
4. The Senate shall elect a Presiding Officer (Chair) from among its members; the office of Chair does not create an additional seat.
5. This allocation shall be reviewed every 20 years by a Constitutional Convention. Numbers may be adjusted only by constitutional amendment, but no nation may

have fewer than its minimum guaranteed seats.

6. Senators shall be nominated by an independent Appointments Commission, constituted by law, and drawn from:
   - Civic Year and national service alumni.
   - Civil society and community leadership.
   - Recognised experts in law, science, economics, culture, and public service.
7. The Commission must ensure that each nation's delegation reflects the diversity of its population, geography, and experience.
8. Senators shall serve a single, non-renewable term of ten years.
9. The Senate shall elect its Presiding Officer (Chair), who presides impartially and represents the chamber in its dealings with the Commons, the Head of State, and the courts.
10. The Senate's principal functions are:
    - Reviewing and revising legislation.
    - Acting as guardian of constitutional fidelity and the unity of the Kingdom.
    - Providing mandatory consent for constitutional amendments, extensions of emergency powers, and other entrenched legislation.

Section 4 - Lawmaking Process

1. A Bill may be introduced in either House, except Money Bills, which must originate in the Commons.
2. A Bill is passed when both Houses approve it in the same form.
3. If the Senate rejects or amends a Bill, the Commons may reconsider.
4. If the Commons passes the Bill a second time, and the Senate rejects it again, the Commons may override by a two-thirds majority within six months, except for entrenched legislation (constitutional amendments,

emergency powers, electoral law), which requires Senate consent.

5. Once passed, the Bill is promulgated by the Head of State and becomes law.

Section 5 - Money Bills and Finance

1. Money Bills include taxation, appropriation, and borrowing measures.
2. Money Bills must originate in the Commons.
3. The Senate may delay but not veto Money Bills beyond 30 days.

Section 6 - Integrity and Transparency

1. All proceedings of both Houses shall be open to the public, except in cases of national security as defined by law.
2. Members of both Houses must disclose financial interests and potential conflicts.
3. Lobbying shall be regulated by statute; gifts, donations, and external income must be disclosed in real time.
4. The Electoral Commission and Civic Integrity Office are entrenched constitutional bodies responsible for oversight of elections, referendums, and political finance.
5. Breach of integrity rules shall be grounds for removal from office, by process defined in statute and subject to judicial review.

Section 7 - Parliamentary Privilege

1. Members of both Houses shall enjoy freedom of speech in Parliament; such speech shall not be questioned in any court.
2. Privilege does not extend to corruption, bribery, or incitement to violence.

3. Each House may discipline its members for misconduct, consistent with due process.

Section 8 - Dissolution and Elections

1. The Commons shall serve a fixed term of four years.
2. Early dissolution may occur only if:
    - A motion of no confidence is passed and no alternative government is confirmed within 30 days; or
    - Parliament votes for early dissolution by a two-thirds majority.
3. Elections shall be held within 60 days of dissolution.

ARTICLE 5 - THE EXECUTIVE

Section 1 - Establishment

1. Executive authority is vested in the Prime Minister and the Council of Ministers (Cabinet), who are collectively responsible to the House of Commons.
2. The executive serves to implement laws, administer government, and safeguard the Constitution, subject always to the limits of law and parliamentary accountability.

Section 2 - The Prime Minister

1. The Prime Minister shall be designated by the House of Commons.
2. The Prime Minister must at all times command the confidence of the Commons.
3. The Prime Minister directs the Council of Ministers, represents the government before Parliament, and coordinates national policy.
4. The Prime Minister may be removed:
    - By a motion of no confidence passed by a simple majority of the Commons; or

   - By resignation.

5. In the event of vacancy, the Commons shall designate a successor within 14 days; otherwise, a general election shall be called.

Section 3 - The Council of Ministers

1. Ministers are appointed by the Prime Minister and approved by the Commons.
2. Ministers must be citizens of the United Kingdom and may be drawn from either House of Parliament or from outside Parliament.
3. Ministers are individually accountable for the actions of their departments and collectively accountable for the policies of the government.
4. Ministers shall not, during their time in office:
   - Engage in private business, investment, or other financial pursuits for profit.
   - Retain direct management of personal property portfolios, businesses, or financial assets, which must be placed in a blind trust or transferred to independent management for the duration of office.
   - Accept personal gifts, funding, or benefits from lobbyists, corporations, or private interest groups.
   - Hold paid positions in any private or public organisation outside their ministerial role.
5. Breach of these provisions shall constitute grounds for dismissal and may be prosecuted as an offence under law.

Section 4 - Ministerial Responsibility

1. Ministers must answer questions before Parliament and provide documents and testimony to committees, except where disclosure would pose a genuine risk to national security, subject to judicial oversight.
2. Misleading Parliament is grounds for removal from office.

3. Abuse of power, corruption, conflicts of interest, or serious misconduct shall constitute offences enforceable by law.
4. The Office of Public Trust shall monitor ministerial compliance with financial and ethical rules, with powers to audit, investigate, and refer breaches for prosecution.

Section 5 - Civil Service

1. A permanent, impartial Civil Service shall serve the government of the day with professionalism, integrity, and political neutrality.
2. Appointments and promotions in the Civil Service shall be made on merit, under procedures established by law.
3. Civil servants shall owe their ultimate duty to the Constitution and the people, not to any party or individual.

Section 6 - War and Treaty Powers

1. The government may not commit armed forces to sustained military action without prior approval of the Commons, except in cases of urgent self-defence.
2. Where urgent action is taken, the government must seek parliamentary approval within seven days.
3. All treaties and international agreements require approval of both Houses before ratification.
4. No treaty may override this Constitution.

Section 7 - Emergency Executive Powers

1. The executive may exercise temporary emergency powers in times of crisis only under conditions authorised by this Constitution.
2. Emergency measures must be:
   - Declared publicly.

  - Time-limited to 90 days, renewable only by a two-thirds vote in both Houses.
  - Subject to review by the Constitutional Court and the Civic Senate.

3. Under no circumstances may emergency powers suspend elections, habeas corpus, due process, or peaceful dissent.

Section 8 - Accountability and Oversight

1. The executive shall be subject to investigation and audit by the Office of Public Trust and by parliamentary committees.
2. Ministers and senior officials may be summoned before the Commons or Senate to give evidence under oath.
3. Misuse of office is grounds for prosecution; no minister or Prime Minister enjoys immunity from criminal law.

ARTICLE 6 - THE JUDICIARY & CONSTITUTIONAL REVIEW

Section 1 - Judicial Independence

1. The judiciary shall be independent of the legislature and executive.
2. Judges shall be subject only to this Constitution and the law.
3. No person or institution may interfere with judicial decision-making.
4. Judges may be removed only for incapacity or serious misconduct, and only upon recommendation of an independent tribunal confirmed by a two-thirds vote of both Houses.

Section 2 - Structure of the Courts

1. The court system shall include:

- Local and regional courts, for civil and criminal matters.
- National courts of appeal.
- The Supreme Court of the United Kingdom, which shall sit as the Constitutional Court when ruling on constitutional questions.

2. Parliament may establish specialised courts (e.g., commercial, family, environmental) by statute, provided they comply with this Constitution.

Section 3 - Constitutional Court Jurisdiction

The Constitutional Court shall have authority to:

1. Review Acts of Parliament, executive actions, and devolved legislation for compatibility with this Constitution.
2. Strike down unconstitutional provisions, with power to issue suspended declarations to allow corrective legislation.
3. Resolve disputes between the UK government and devolved nations, or between devolved institutions.
4. Rule on the validity of referendums, elections, and amendment procedures.
5. Provide advisory opinions when requested by Parliament or the Head of State.

Section 4 - Judicial Appointments

1. Judges of the Constitutional Court and senior national courts shall be appointed by the Head of State on the recommendation of an independent Judicial Appointments Commission (JAC).
2. The JAC shall consist of representatives from the judiciary, legal profession, academia, and civil society, appointed in a transparent process.
3. Criteria for appointment shall include legal excellence,

integrity, independence, and commitment to constitutional values, with regard for gender and regional balance.

4. Terms of office for Constitutional Court judges shall be 12 years, non-renewable.

Section 5 - Access to Justice

1. Everyone has the right to a fair hearing before an independent and impartial tribunal within a reasonable time.
2. Legal aid shall be provided by the state where necessary to ensure equal access to justice.
3. Standing rules shall allow individuals, groups, and organisations to bring cases in the public interest, including challenges to unconstitutional laws or practices.
4. Court fees must be reasonable and not a barrier to justice.

Section 6 - Judicial Accountability

1. Judges are subject to the same laws as other citizens.
2. Judicial proceedings and judgments shall be public, except in limited cases of privacy or security, as prescribed by law.
3. Judges must publish reasons for their decisions.
4. A Judicial Conduct Board, established by statute, shall investigate complaints of misconduct and recommend action.

Section 7 - Limits of Judicial Power in Sovereignty, Security, and Borders

1. Courts shall have jurisdiction to ensure that asylum, immigration, and deportation laws comply with this

Constitution and with international obligations expressly ratified by the United Kingdom.

2. Courts shall not create or extend rights beyond those set out in this Constitution or ratified by law.
3. Where Parliament has enacted clear and lawful provisions for:
   - The removal or deportation of persons who have no legal right to remain; or
   - The detention or removal of individuals who pose a threat to public safety, national security, or civic order.

   Courts shall not prevent their enforcement, except where such provisions directly violate non-derogable rights under this Constitution.
4. In interpreting asylum and immigration law, courts shall give due weight to:
   - The sovereignty of the people.
   - The duty of the state to preserve public safety, cohesion, and integrity of borders; and
   - The democratic authority of Parliament in setting national policy.
5. Where doubt arises, courts shall resolve conflicts in a manner that preserves both individual dignity and the security of the nation.

ARTICLE 7 - DEVOLUTION & LOCAL GOVERNMENT

Section 1 - Principles of Devolution

1. The United Kingdom is a union of nations; England, Scotland, Wales, and Northern Ireland - each with the right to self-government within the framework of this Constitution.
2. All powers are devolved by default, except those expressly reserved in Schedule A.
3. Devolved governments shall exercise their powers in a manner consistent with this Constitution and with the sovereignty of the people.

4. Local government is recognised as a constitutionally protected level of governance, with powers that cannot be removed except by constitutional amendment.

Section 1A – Admission of New Nations

1. Additional nations or territories may be admitted to the United Kingdom by:
    - A request from the people of the territory, expressed through a democratic referendum.
    - Approval by a two-thirds majority in both Houses of Parliament; and
    - Ratification by a majority vote in a national referendum of the United Kingdom.
2. Upon admission, the new nation shall enjoy self-government within the framework of this Constitution, be guaranteed representation in the Civic Senate, and hold the same rights, duties, and protections as the existing nations of the Union.
3. Parliament shall by law determine the transitional arrangements necessary for the integration of new nations into the Union, consistent with this Constitution.

Section 2 - National Legislatures and Executives

1. Scotland, Wales, and Northern Ireland shall each have a legislature and an executive government, elected under systems determined by their constitutions, consistent with democratic principles.
2. England may, by law, establish devolved regional assemblies or councils.
3. Devolved legislatures may legislate on all matters not reserved, including health, education, housing, policing, transport, environment, and culture.
4. The executives of devolved governments shall be accountable to their legislatures.

Section 3 - Consent and the Sewel Principle

1. The UK Parliament shall not legislate with respect to devolved matters without the consent of the relevant devolved legislature.
2. Any law passed without such consent shall be inoperative in that nation unless approved by:
   - A two-thirds majority of both Houses of Parliament; and
   - A confirmatory referendum in the affected nation.
3. This principle shall be legally binding and justiciable before the Constitutional Court.

Section 4 - Northern Ireland

1. The institutions of Northern Ireland shall operate in accordance with the Belfast/Good Friday Agreement and its successors.
2. Any change to Northern Ireland's constitutional status requires the consent of a majority of its people in a referendum.
3. Cross-community consent rules for key decisions shall be constitutionally guaranteed.

Section 5 - Intergovernmental Relations

1. An Intergovernmental Council shall be established, composed of representatives from the UK government and devolved governments, to coordinate policy and manage disputes.
2. The Council shall:
   - Meet regularly to discuss shared issues (infrastructure, environment, economic policy, security).
   - Provide a forum for negotiation and cooperation.
   - Refer unresolved disputes to binding mediation, and, if necessary, to the Constitutional Court.

3. Decisions of the Council shall be published, except where national security requires confidentiality.

Section 6 - Local Government

1. Local councils shall have constitutionally protected powers of taxation, spending, and law-making on matters of local concern.
2. Local authorities shall:
    - Control core infrastructure spending within their area.
    - Conduct participatory budgeting processes with citizens.
    - Be subject to annual review by local citizen panels.
3. No devolved or UK government may abolish or override local government except as provided by constitutional amendment.

Section 7 - Finance and Fiscal Autonomy

1. Devolved governments may levy taxes, borrow, and manage budgets for devolved matters, consistent with national fiscal rules.
2. A system of fair fiscal transfers shall be established to ensure that every nation and region of the UK can provide a comparable standard of public service.
3. The Office of Budget Responsibility shall oversee intergovernmental finance to ensure fairness and transparency.

Section 8 - Judicial Review of Devolution

1. The Constitutional Court shall have authority to resolve disputes concerning:
    - The division of reserved and devolved powers.
    - Alleged breaches of the Sewel consent requirement.

- Disputes between devolved governments and the UK government.

2. In case of doubt, interpretation shall favour the devolved level of government, unless a matter is expressly reserved.

Section 9 - Union Collaboration through the Senate

1. Each devolved nation's Senators in the Civic Senate shall serve as a link between devolved legislatures and Parliament.
2. Senate committees shall include representatives from every nation to review UK-wide issues such as:
   - Shared infrastructure projects.
   - Environmental protection and climate policy.
   - National security and resilience.
   - Intergovernmental finance and fair fiscal transfers.
3. In this way, the Senate shall act as a chamber of union, ensuring that the voices of all nations are represented in national decision-making.

ARTICLE 8 - ELECTIONS & REFERENDUMS

Section 1 - General Principles

1. Elections and referendums shall be conducted freely, fairly, and transparently, under impartial administration.
2. The franchise shall be universal, equal, and secret. Every eligible citizen shall have an equal vote of equal value.
3. The conduct of elections and referendums shall be overseen by an independent Electoral Commission, entrenched under this Constitution.

Section 2 - The Franchise

1. Every citizen of the United Kingdom aged 18 or above shall have the right to vote in elections and referendums.

2. Citizens aged 16 or above shall gain the right to vote early if they:
    - Have paid income tax or National Insurance contributions; or
    - Have completed a recognised period of national or civic service.
3. Naturalised citizens shall be enfranchised upon completion of their Civic Year of national service, regardless of age.
4. The right to vote shall not be denied on the basis of race, sex, gender, language, religion, belief, disability, sexual orientation, or economic status.
5. Any restriction on voting (such as in cases of imprisonment for serious offences) must be proportionate, time-limited, and subject to review.

Section 3 - The Right to Stand for Office

1. Every citizen aged 18 or above shall have the right to stand for elected office, provided they have completed their Civic Year of national service.
2. Naturalised citizens shall be eligible to stand for office once they have:
    - Completed their Civic Year; and
    - Held citizenship for at least five years.
3. Citizens disqualified for reasons of serious criminal conviction, corruption, or breach of constitutional duties may be barred from candidacy by law.
4. No citizen shall be excluded from candidacy on grounds of wealth, belief, or political affiliation.

Section 4 - Electoral Boundaries and Constituencies

1. Electoral boundaries shall be determined by an independent Boundaries Commission, applying objective criteria of population equality, geography, and community ties.

2. Boundaries shall be reviewed at least every ten years.
3. The Boundaries Commission shall act independently of Parliament and political parties.

Section 5 - Administration of Elections

1. The Electoral Commission shall:
    - Register voters and maintain a national electoral roll.
    - Supervise polling, counting, and certification of results.
    - Ensure accessibility for all citizens, including persons with disabilities.
    - Guarantee transparency and security in voting technologies.
2. Electronic voting, if used, must be verifiable, auditable, and resistant to interference.

Section 6 - Campaign Finance and Political Integrity

1. All donations to political parties, candidates, or campaigns must be publicly disclosed in real time.
2. Donations from foreign sources, corporations not operating in the UK, or anonymous donors are prohibited.
3. Expenditure limits shall be set by law and enforced by the Electoral Commission.
4. Lobbying activity shall be transparent and subject to statutory regulation.
5. Breaches of campaign finance law are grounds for disqualification of candidates and annulment of election results.

Section 7 - Referendums

1. Referendums shall be held on constitutional matters,

sovereignty issues, or as required by this Constitution.

2. The rules for referendums shall be set by an Independent Referendum Act, consistent with this Constitution, and supervised by the Electoral Commission.
3. Referendum campaigns must be publicly funded on an equal basis, with strict spending limits.
4. Neutral information and accessible materials must be provided to all voters.
5. Constitutional referendums shall require:
    - A simple majority of valid votes cast, and
    - At least a majority in three of the four nations of the United Kingdom, unless otherwise specified in the amendment procedure.
6. Parliament may provide for turnout or supermajority thresholds by law, provided these are set in advance and apply equally to all sides.

Section 8 - Right to Challenge Results

1. Election and referendum results may be challenged in court by candidates, parties, or citizens, on grounds of fraud, corruption, or breach of law.
2. The Constitutional Court shall have final jurisdiction over such challenges.

ARTICLE 9 - FINANCE & ACCOUNTABILITY

Section 1 - Principles of Public Finance

1. All public money belongs to the people and shall be used only in accordance with this Constitution and laws made under it.
2. Public finance shall be governed by the principles of transparency, sustainability, and fairness between generations and regions.
3. No tax, duty, or levy shall be imposed except by law.

4. No public money shall be spent except under the authority of Parliament.

Section 2 - The Budget Process

1. The government shall present an annual budget to the House of Commons, setting out expected revenue and expenditure for the coming financial year.
2. The budget shall include a medium-term fiscal framework of at least three years.
3. The Commons shall debate, amend, and vote on the budget; the Senate may review and propose revisions but cannot veto.
4. If Parliament fails to pass a budget before the start of the financial year, temporary funding at the previous year's levels shall continue until a new budget is enacted.

Section 3 - Borrowing and Fiscal Responsibility

1. The government may borrow only within limits set by law and consistent with long-term fiscal sustainability.
2. Borrowing shall not impose an unreasonable burden on future generations.
3. The Office for Budget Responsibility (OBR) shall review and publish independent assessments of government borrowing and debt.
4. Any extraordinary borrowing beyond statutory limits requires approval by a two-thirds majority in both Houses.

Section 4 - Audit and Oversight

1. The National Audit Office (NAO) shall audit all public accounts annually and report directly to Parliament.
2. The NAO shall have full access to government departments, public bodies, and contractors receiving public funds.

3. Audit findings must be published in full, except where national security requires limited redaction.
4. Parliament must debate NAO reports within 60 days of publication.

Section 5 - Integrity in Public Office

1. All public officials, elected or appointed, shall declare assets, income, and financial interests annually.
2. Ministers and senior officials must place significant private assets into blind trusts or divestment during their term.
3. No public official shall receive personal funding, gifts, or benefits from lobbyists, corporations, or foreign governments.
4. Breach of financial integrity provisions constitutes grounds for removal and may be prosecuted as a criminal offence.

Section 6 - Freedom of Information and Transparency

1. Every person has the right to access information held by public authorities, subject only to limited restrictions necessary for national security or personal privacy.
2. Public contracts, procurement processes, and spending over a threshold set by law shall be published in full.
3. The Information Commissioner shall oversee and enforce the right to information, with powers to compel disclosure.

Section 7 - Anti-Corruption Safeguards

1. The Office of Public Trust shall have powers to:
    - Audit all branches of government annually.
    - Investigate corruption or abuse of power.
    - Subpoena documents and testimony.
    - Pause or review policies under investigation.

  - Refer cases for prosecution.

2. The Office shall act independently, with commissioners appointed by a multi-party supermajority and removable only for cause.

Section 8 - Public Procurement Integrity

1. All contracts for goods, services, or works exceeding a threshold set by law shall be awarded through transparent, competitive processes.
2. Full contract terms, including costs and modifications, must be published within 30 days of signing, subject only to limited redactions for national security.
3. An independent authority, established under the Office of Public Trust, shall:
   - Review major contracts against market standards.
   - Audit performance and delivery.
   - Report annually to Parliament on value for money in public procurement.
4. Any contract found to involve fraud, collusion, or gross overcharging shall be declared voidable, with restitution owed to the public treasury.
5. Firms or individuals found guilty of corrupt practices in public procurement shall:
   - Be barred from future government contracts for a period set by law.
   - Repay unlawfully obtained profits.
   - Be subject to prosecution under anti-corruption law.
6. Citizens' panels may be convened to review and advise on mega-projects above a threshold set by law, ensuring public participation and oversight.

ARTICLE 10 - SECURITY & EMERGENCIES

Section 1 - Principles of Security

1. Security services and armed forces exist to protect the people, the Constitution, and the democratic order, not to rule over them.

2. All security powers shall be exercised under law, subject to parliamentary and judicial oversight.
3. The preservation of liberty and dignity shall remain the guiding principle even in times of crisis.

Section 2 - Policing

1. Policing in the United Kingdom shall be based on the principle of policing by consent.
2. Police services shall be locally accountable but coordinated nationally to address cross-border crime and threats.
   - Use of force must be:
   - Necessary.
   - Proportionate, and
   - Subject to independent investigation where serious harm occurs.
3. Parliament shall establish independent Police Oversight Authorities in each nation of the UK, empowered to investigate misconduct, abuse, or corruption.

Section 3 - Intelligence Services

1. Intelligence services shall operate only under statute and within the limits of this Constitution.
2. All surveillance or interception must:
   - Be authorised by a judge.
   - Be necessary for national security or the prevention of serious crime,
   - Be proportionate, and
   - Be time-limited.
3. Parliamentary oversight committees, drawn from both Houses, shall review intelligence operations regularly.
4. Whistleblowers exposing abuse of intelligence powers shall be protected by law.

Section 4 - Armed Forces

1. The armed forces shall defend the United Kingdom against external threats, assist in emergencies, and support allies under lawfully approved treaties.
2. The armed forces shall remain politically neutral and under civilian control at all times.
3. Deployment of the armed forces in domestic operations shall be lawful only:
   - At the request of civil authorities.
   - Where proportionate to the emergency.
   - Subject to review by Parliament and the courts.

Section 5 - Emergency Powers

1. Emergency powers may be declared only in cases of:
   - War or armed attack.
   - Natural disaster of exceptional scale.
   - Systemic collapse of essential infrastructure.
   - Internal insurrection threatening the survival of the Constitution.
2. An emergency must be publicly declared by the government, specifying scope, duration, and justification.
3. Emergency powers are time-limited to 90 days, and may only be extended by a two-thirds vote in both Houses.
4. All emergency measures remain subject to:
   - Judicial review.
   - Oversight by the Civic Senate.
   - Audit by the Office of Public Trust.

Section 6 - Prohibited Measures

Even during an emergency, it shall be prohibited to:

- Suspend or cancel scheduled elections.
- Abolish habeas corpus or due process.
- Permit indefinite detention without trial.
- Suspend the Bill of Rights.
- Censor or intimidate the press.

- Criminalise peaceful protest or dissent.

Section 7 - Sunset and Accountability

1. All emergency powers expire automatically at the end of their declared period.
2. No emergency power may be made permanent, nor used to amend or suspend this Constitution.
3. Within six months of the end of an emergency, Parliament shall publish a full report on the measures taken, their necessity, and their consequences.
4. Officials found to have abused emergency powers shall be held personally accountable before the law.

ARTICLE 11 - INDEPENDENT INTEGRITY BODIES

Section 1 - Principles

1. Independent integrity bodies exist to safeguard the Constitution, protect democracy, and defend public trust.
2. They shall operate transparently, impartially, and free from influence by government, parties, or private interests.
3. Their independence is constitutionally guaranteed. Their budgets shall be set by Parliament on a multi-party basis and may not be reduced to impair their functioning.

Section 2 - The Office of Public Trust

1. The Office of Public Trust is a permanent constitutional body tasked with:
    - Auditing all branches of government and major public bodies annually.

  - Investigating corruption, misconduct, or abuse of power.
  - Subpoenaing documents and testimony in pursuit of its duties.
  - Pausing or suspending policies under investigation until review is complete.
  - Referring cases for prosecution to the appropriate authorities.
2. The Office shall be led by a Commission of Integrity of five members, appointed by a two-thirds majority of both Houses and removable only for incapacity or misconduct confirmed by the Constitutional Court.
3. Reports of the Office shall be published in full, except where redaction is strictly required for national security.
4. Citizens shall have the right to petition the Office with evidence of corruption or abuse, and petitions must be reviewed.

Section 3 - The Electoral Commission

1. The Electoral Commission shall oversee:
   - Voter registration and maintenance of electoral rolls.
   - Supervision of polling, counting, and certification of results.
   - Regulation of political parties, donations, and campaign finance.
   - Supervision of referendums under the Independent Referendum Act.
2. The Commission shall act impartially and transparently, reporting directly to Parliament.
3. Commissioners shall be appointed by a supermajority of both Houses and removable only for cause.

Section 4 - The Civic Integrity Office

1. The Civic Integrity Office shall enforce rules on:

- Lobbying and influence activity.
- Transparency of donations and gifts.
- Conflicts of interest in public service.

2. The Office shall have powers to investigate breaches, impose fines, and refer cases for prosecution.
3. The Office shall publish real-time registers of donations, lobbying activity, and public officials' interests.

Section 5 - The National Audit Office (NAO)

1. The NAO shall audit all public accounts and report directly to Parliament.
2. It shall have full access to government departments, public bodies, and contractors.
3. Its findings must be published in full, and Parliament must debate them within 60 days.

Section 6 - The Office for Budget Responsibility (OBR)

1. The OBR shall provide independent analysis of government borrowing, spending, and debt sustainability.
2. It shall publish forecasts and fiscal assessments at least twice yearly.
3. Its findings shall be binding on government reporting and incorporated into budget debates.

Section 7 - The Information Commissioner

1. The Information Commissioner shall safeguard the right to information and data protection.
2. The Commissioner shall have powers to compel disclosure, enforce data rights, and impose sanctions for breaches.
3. All citizens shall have the right to appeal to the Commissioner when denied access to information.

Section 8 - Judicial Appointments Commission (JAC)

1. The JAC shall recommend appointments to the Constitutional Court and senior judiciary.
2. It shall consist of judges, legal professionals, academics, and civil society representatives, appointed transparently and impartially.
3. Its decisions shall be binding on the Head of State.

Section 9 - Independence and Protection

1. The budgets of all independent integrity bodies shall be approved by a cross-party committee of Parliament, insulated from day-to-day political control.
2. Leaders of these bodies shall be appointed by supermajority and removable only for cause.
3. Any attempt to abolish or undermine these bodies without constitutional amendment shall be void.

ARTICLE 12 - AMENDMENT & REVIEW

Section 1 - Principles

1. This Constitution may be amended, but never casually.
2. The amendment process shall balance flexibility, so the Constitution can evolve with the nation, and stability, so its foundations cannot be dismantled by temporary majorities.
3. No amendment may be adopted without the clear and informed consent of the people.

Section 2 - Proposals for Amendment

1. Amendments may be proposed by:
    - A two-thirds vote of the House of Commons; or
    - A two-thirds vote of the Civic Senate; or
    - A verified petition of at least one million citizens.

2. Citizen petitions shall be reviewed by the Constitutional Court to confirm authenticity and constitutional compatibility before proceeding.

Section 3 - Ratification of Amendments

1. To be ratified, all proposed amendments must:
    - Pass by a two-thirds vote in both the Commons and the Senate; and
    - Be approved in a national referendum by a simple majority of votes cast.
2. Constitutional amendments affecting the powers or status of a particular nation (Scotland, Wales, Northern Ireland, or England's devolved assemblies) shall also require the approval of a majority of voters in that nation.
3. Amendments affecting the Union itself (e.g., secession or dissolution) shall require:
    - A two-thirds vote in both House.
    - A national referendum with at least 60% approval, and
    - Majorities in all four nations of the UK.

Section 4 - Unamendable Clauses (Constitutional Core)

The following principles may not be amended or abolished:

1. Free and fair elections.
2. Core rights listed as non-derogable in Article 3.
3. The independence of the judiciary and Constitutional Court.
4. The constitutional status of devolved governments without their consent.
5. The requirement of parliamentary accountability of the executive.
6. The prohibition on emergency powers being used to suspend this Constitution.

Section 5 - Periodic Review

1. Every 20 years, a Constitutional Convention shall be convened to review the performance and adequacy of this Constitution.
2. The Convention shall consist of:
    - Delegates elected by the people.
    - Citizens chosen by civic lottery.
    - Representatives of service alumni, civil society, and academia.
3. The Convention may recommend amendments, which must then proceed through the ratification process set out in Section 3.
4. Convention proceedings shall be public, broadcast, and recorded as a matter of civic education.

Section 6 - Judicial Safeguards

1. All proposed amendments shall be reviewed by the Constitutional Court for compatibility with the unamendable core.
2. Any amendment found to violate the core shall be void and of no effect.

ARTICLE 13 - TRANSITION

Section 1 - Adoption of the Constitution

1. This Constitution shall be adopted through the following process:
    - A Constitutional Convention convened by Act of Parliament.
    - Approval of the draft Constitution by a two-thirds majority in both the House of Commons and the Civic Senate (or, before their creation, by a joint committee of both Houses).
    - Ratification by the people in a national referendum, by simple majority of votes cast.

2. Upon ratification, this Constitution shall enter into force on a date ("Commencement Day") fixed by Act of Parliament.

Section 2 - Continuity of Law

1. All existing laws, institutions, and offices shall continue in force on Commencement Day, unless and until they are repealed or amended to conform with this Constitution.
2. Within five years of Commencement Day, Parliament shall conduct a comprehensive review of all statutes to align them with constitutional principles.

Section 3 - The Head of State

1. On Commencement Day, the monarchy shall continue as Head of State in ceremonial form, with all prerogative powers abolished.
2. All Crown assets, estates, and revenues shall be placed under a Crown Public Trust, administered by Parliament on behalf of the people.
3. Over the course of twenty years, all Crown assets shall be transferred in stages into permanent public ownership, with management and revenues returning to the people and state.
4. Members of the Royal Family may receive civil allowances during this period, as determined by statute and subject to review by Parliament.
5. Twenty years after Commencement Day, a Constitutional Review shall be held to determine whether to retain the monarchy or transfer its ceremonial functions to a non-executive President.
6. Should abolition of the monarchy be chosen by referendum and supermajority of Parliament, transition shall occur within one year, with all remaining Crown assets fully absorbed into state ownership.

Section 4 - The Legislature

1. On Commencement Day, the House of Lords shall be dissolved.
2. The Civic Senate shall be constituted within twelve months, with its first members appointed by the independent Appointments Commission under transitional legislation.
3. Until the Senate is seated, its functions under this Constitution shall be performed by a joint committee of both Houses.

Section 5 - The Civic Year

1. The National Civic Service Authority shall be established within two years of Commencement Day to design and administer the Civic Year programme.
2. Mandatory Civic Year service shall begin no later than five years after Commencement Day, phased by annual cohorts.
3. Full civic rights (standing for office, senior public positions, state honours) shall be tied to completion of the Civic Year once the programme is fully operational.

Section 6 - Judiciary and Constitutional Court

1. The Supreme Court of the United Kingdom shall assume the role of Constitutional Court on Commencement Day.
2. Transitional provisions shall allow existing Justices to serve until retirement, subject to the new rules of appointment and tenure.
3. The Judicial Appointments Commission shall be established within one year of Commencement Day.

Section 7 - Independent Integrity Bodies

1. The Electoral Commission, National Audit Office, Office

for Budget Responsibility, and Information Commissioner shall continue in force and become constitutionally entrenched immediately on Commencement Day.

2. The Office of Public Trust and the Civic Integrity Office shall be established by law within two years of Commencement Day.
3. These bodies shall assume full constitutional powers once created.

Section 8 - Devolution and Reserved Powers

1. The devolved governments of Scotland, Wales, and Northern Ireland shall continue in force with their current powers until revised legislation aligns them with this Constitution.
2. Schedule A (Reserved Powers) shall come into immediate effect on Commencement Day.
3. Disputes concerning competence arising during the transition shall be resolved by the Constitutional Court.

Section 9 - Emergencies During Transition

1. No emergency power shall be used to delay or suspend the commencement of this Constitution.
2. Any attempt to do so shall be void and unlawful.

Section 10 - Civic Education

1. Within two years of Commencement Day, Parliament shall establish a national programme of civic education to ensure that every citizen understands the rights, duties, and structures of this Constitution.
2. Copies of the Constitution shall be provided free of charge to every school, library, and household, and made available online.

Schedule A - Reserved Powers

The following matters are reserved to the United Kingdom government and Parliament. All other matters are devolved to the nations and local governments.

1. The Constitution and Civic Order

- The Constitution of the United Kingdom.
- Succession, Head of State, and national symbols.
- Civil Service and Crown appointments.
- Treason and offences against the state.

2. Foreign Affairs and International Relations

- Diplomacy and recognition of states.
- International treaties, alliances, and membership of international organisations.
- Foreign aid and international development.
- Defence of citizens abroad.

3. Defence and National Security

- Armed forces and military bases.
- Nuclear weapons and strategic deterrence.
- Intelligence services.
- Defence procurement and arms export controls.
- National security strategy.

4. Fiscal, Monetary and Economic Policy

- Currency, coinage, and the Bank of England.
- Monetary policy, exchange rate, and government borrowing/lending.
- Inheritance tax, corporation tax, VAT, excise duties, motoring taxation.
- National Insurance, capital gains tax, income tax on savings and dividends.

- Pensions and state benefits relating to retirement.
- Financial services and markets regulation.

5. Justice, Order and Civic Integrity

- Drug policy and classification of controlled substances.
- Firearms regulation.
- Data protection and privacy standards.
- Betting, gaming, and lotteries.
- Immigration, nationality, and citizenship.

6. Commerce, Competition and Consumer Protection

- Competition law and consumer protection.
- Intellectual property, patents, trademarks, copyright.
- Import and export control.
- Product standards, weights and measures.
- Common markets for goods and services across the UK.

7. Infrastructure, Energy and Communications

- Telecommunications and spectrum allocation.
- Postal services.
- Broadcasting, including the BBC and national networks.
- Electricity, coal, oil, gas, and nuclear energy policy.
- Large-scale cross-border infrastructure.

8. Employment and Industrial Relations

- Employment law and minimum standards.
- Health and safety regulation.
- Trade union law and collective bargaining rights.

9. Transport Safety and Regulation

- Aviation, shipping, and railway safety.
- National transport security.

- Standards for motor vehicles and road traffic regulation at UK level.

10. Social Security and National Welfare

- Universal Credit and its predecessor schemes.
- Jobseeker's Allowance, Income Support, Housing Benefit.
- Child Benefit, Child Tax Credit, Working Tax Credit.
- National insurance contributions and entitlements.

Closing Declaration

I speak to the people to remind them that the role of this Constitution is to engrave rights in stone, but not to fix forever the methods by which those rights are secured. The purpose of government, and of this Constitution, is the defence of the liberty, welfare, and dignity of the British people. If in time any article or amendment should prove withered by age, or shown by experience to hinder the common good, then the spirit of this Constitution invites renewal. For its strength lies not in rigidity, but in its living bond with the people it serves.

Afterword

In a time of extremes, where we as British people are becoming more disconnected from one another, we need to come back to the middle ground. We need to come back to a shared truth.

Our enemies have never been more empowered. Our allies have never been more discouraged. We need to start from the beginning and agree on principled values and truths so we can build again. That our children should grow up in a better world than the one we were left. That justice should serve everyone, not just the richest. That freedom means duty as well as right. That dignity belongs to all, or it belongs to none.

If something does not change, we will lose.

But there is a reason the wolves must come at us from so many sides at once to try and overwhelm us. It is because we are not the underdog in this story. The British people, our tradition, our spirit, hold the potential for the greatest good and the greatest strength.

When the Vikings raided our shores, we built the finest navy the world had ever seen. When the Nazis came knocking on the door of Europe, we did not hesitate to answer, even when the threat had not yet reached our own soil.

I wrote this book because I worry. I look at the streets of Gateshead, where I campaign for change, and I see the abandonment of a region. I see rising poverty, rising addiction among the young, and fewer alternatives to hope. But worst of all, I see the spirit of the wolves breaking down the spirit of the sheepdog that every Briton holds in their heart.

Yet I still believe in that spirit. I see it in the teacher who refuses to give up on a child, in the nurse who works another shift, in the neighbour who still checks on the elderly man next door, and in all the great people I meet daily who refuse to surrender. The sheepdog is not gone. It only needs to be called again.

It is the responsibility of Sheepdog Liberals, of all who still believe in Britain's promise, to fight for and win back our nation.

If not now, when?
And if not you, who?

Printed in Dunstable, United Kingdom

71486081R00099